This book belong to:

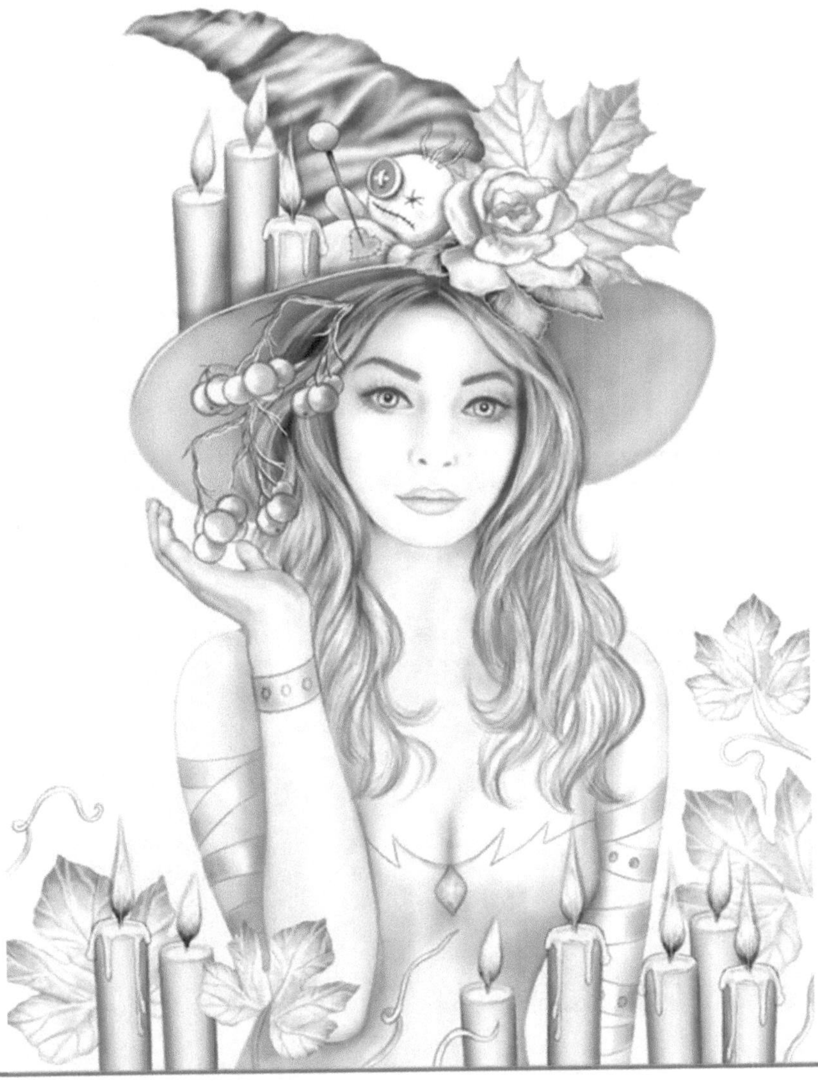

Color Test Page

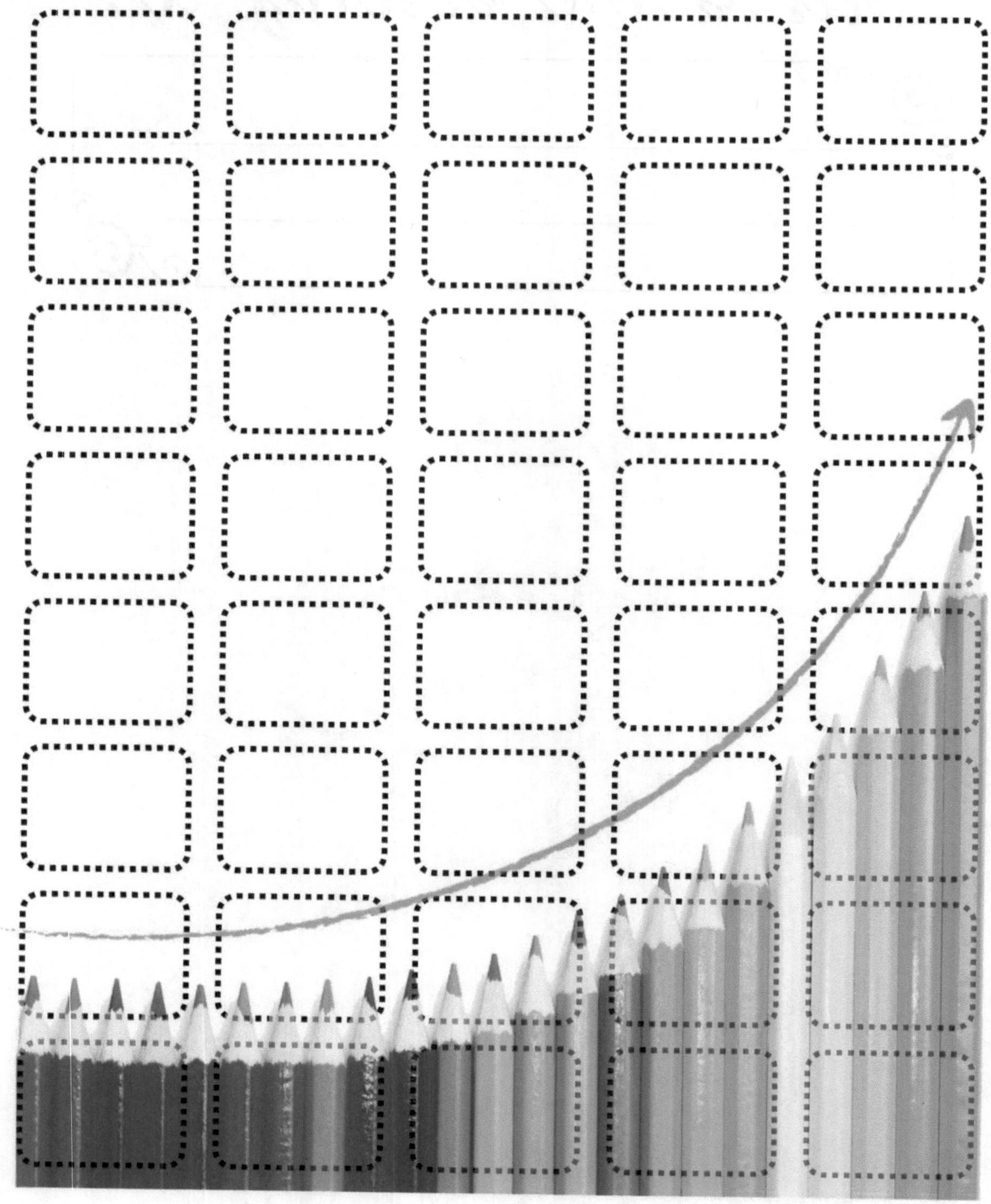

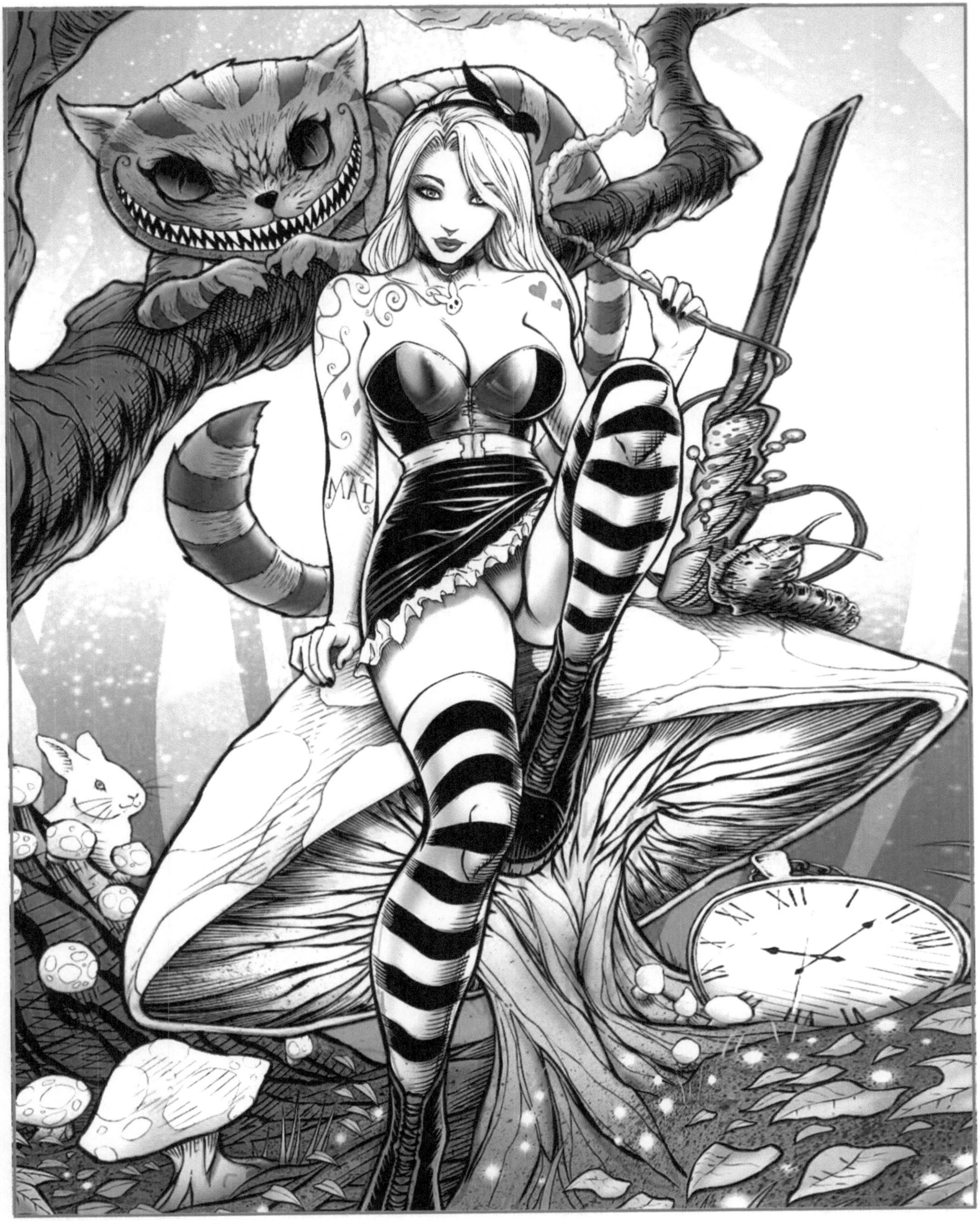

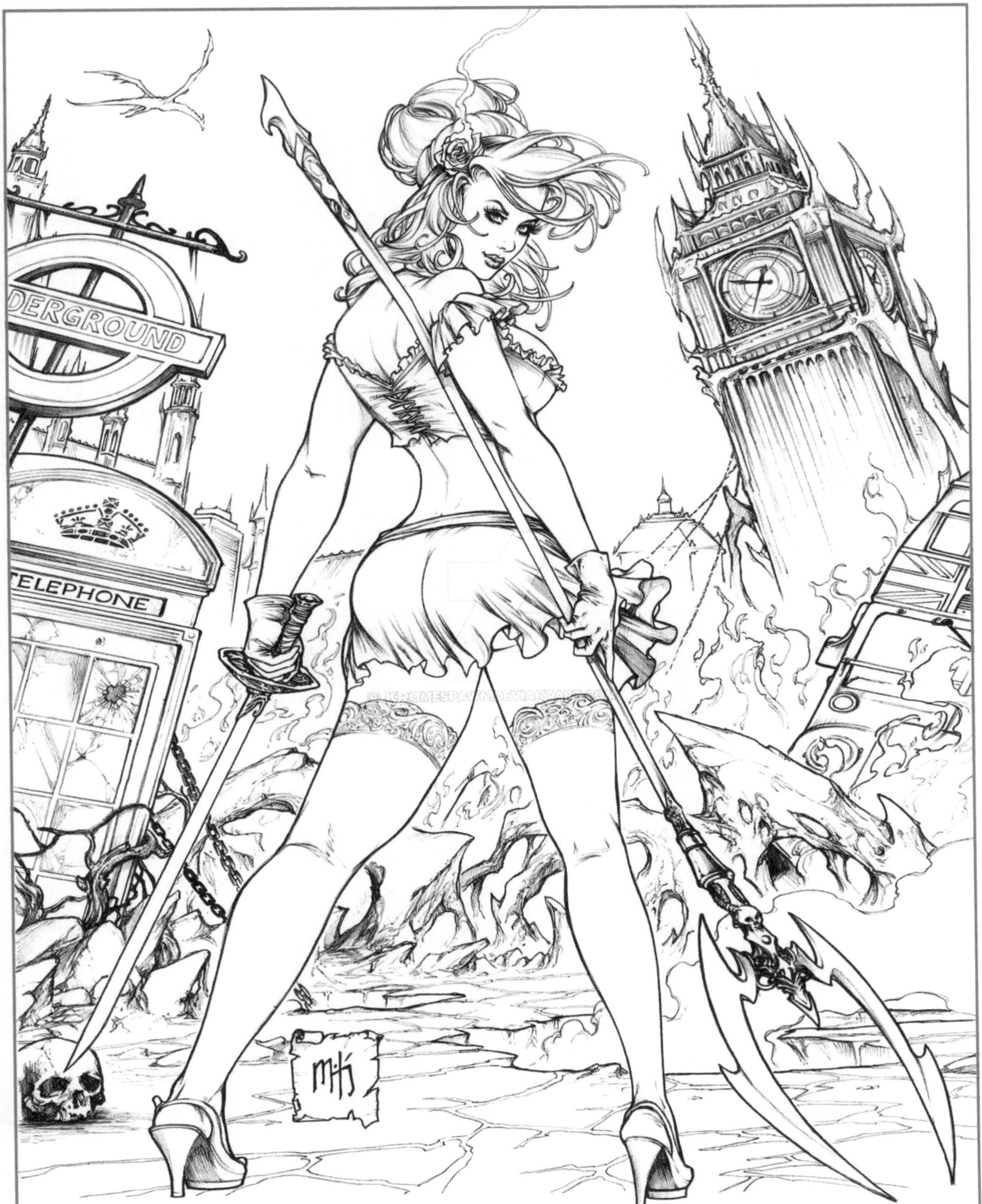
DERGROUND
TELEPHONE

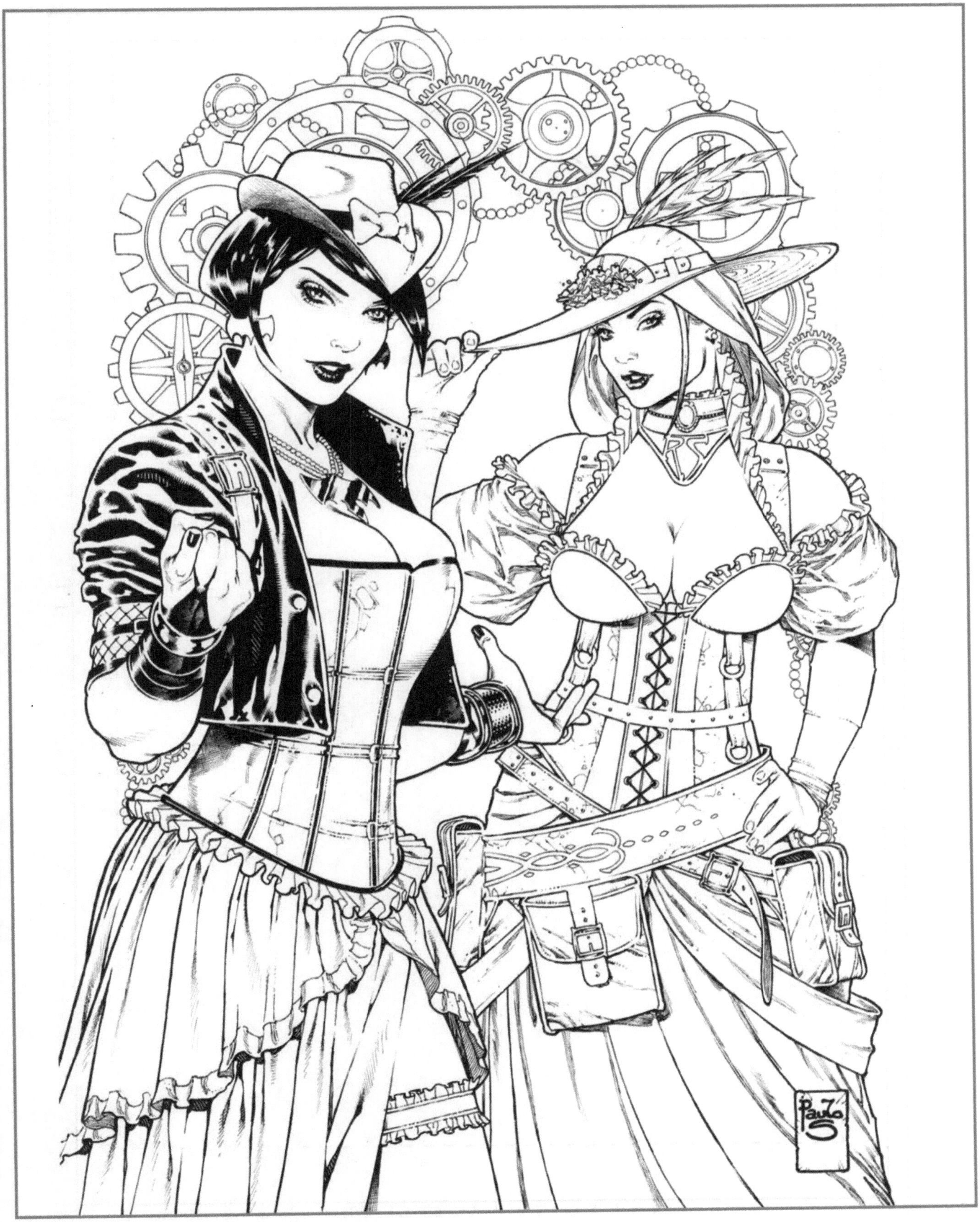
Paulo

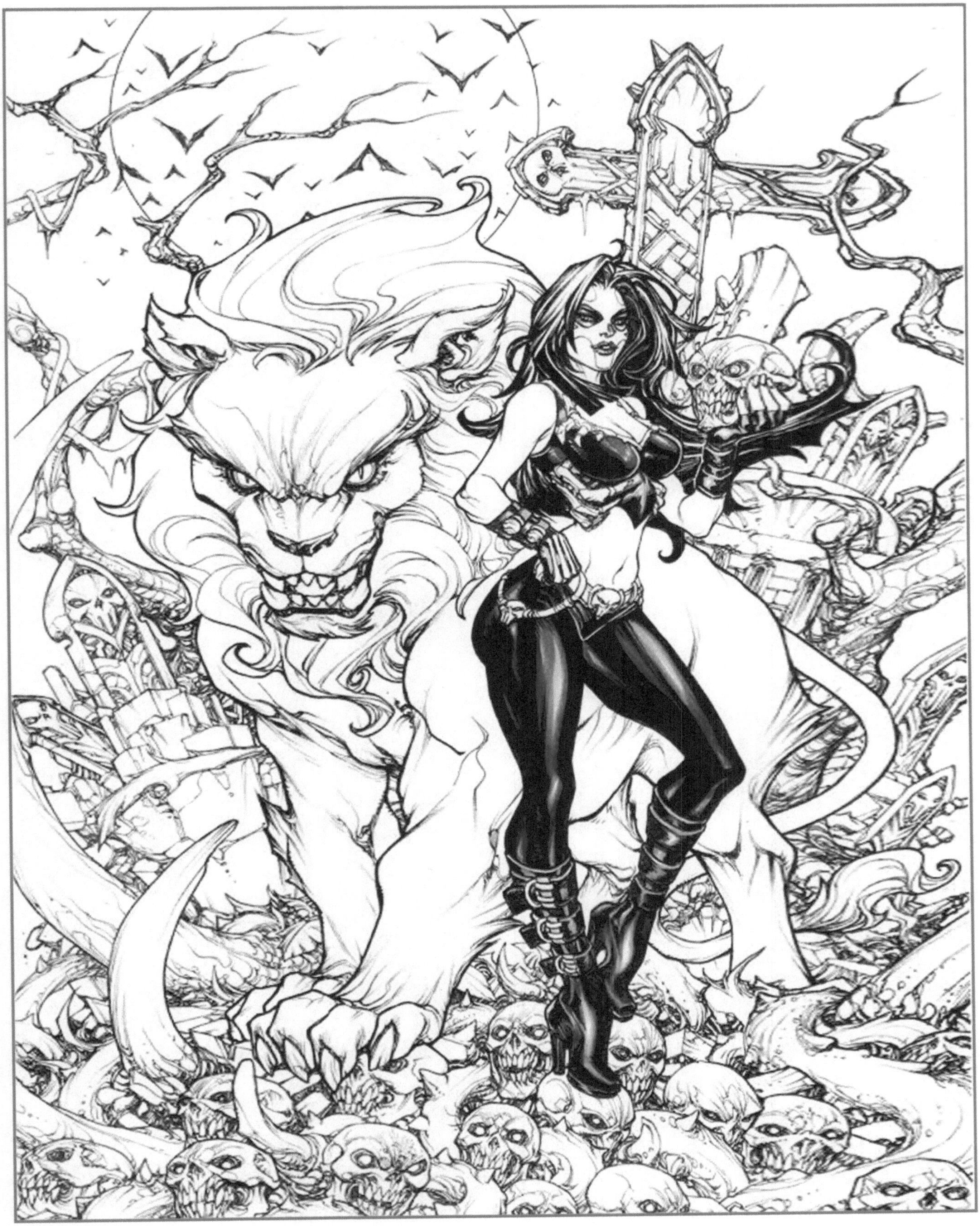

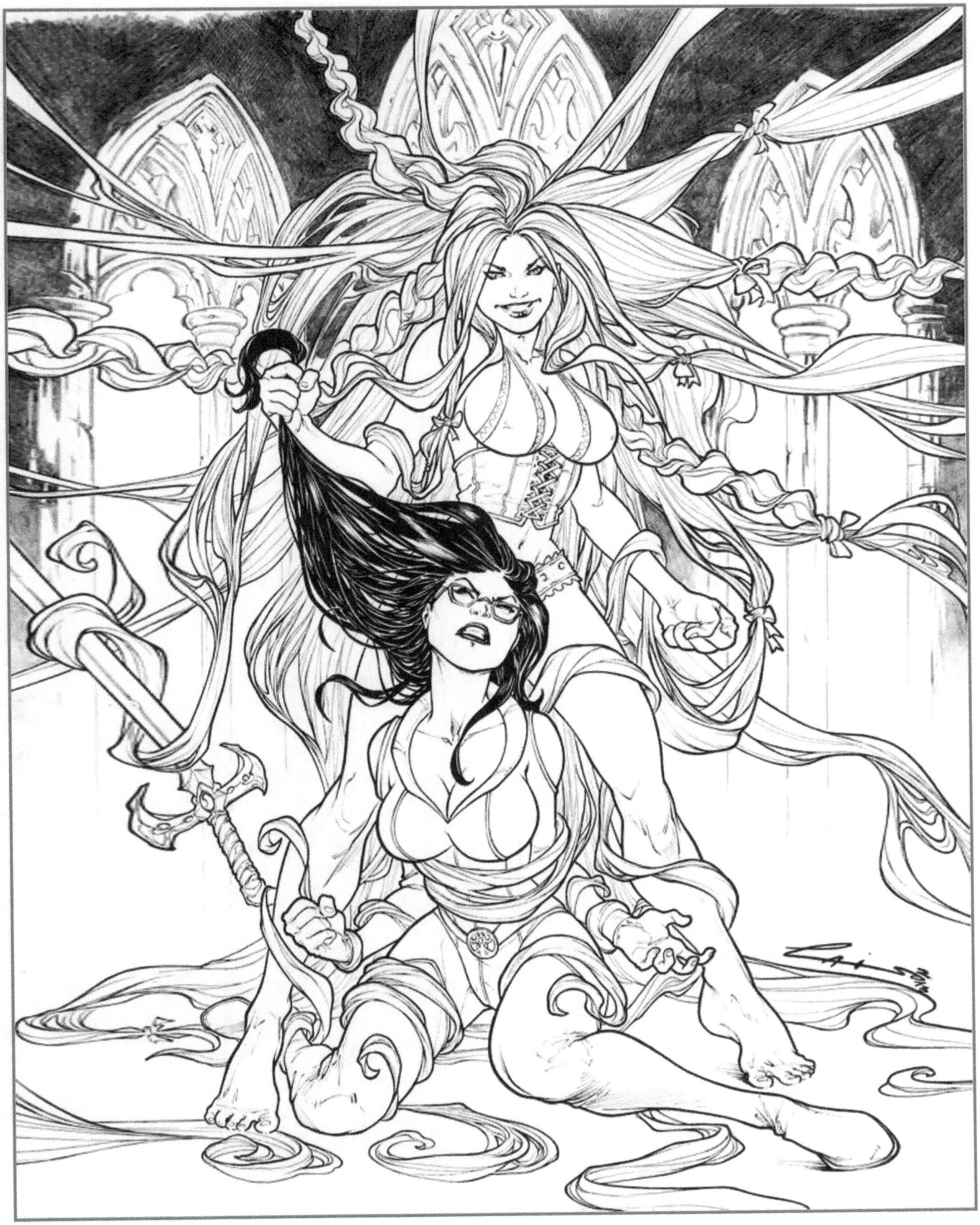

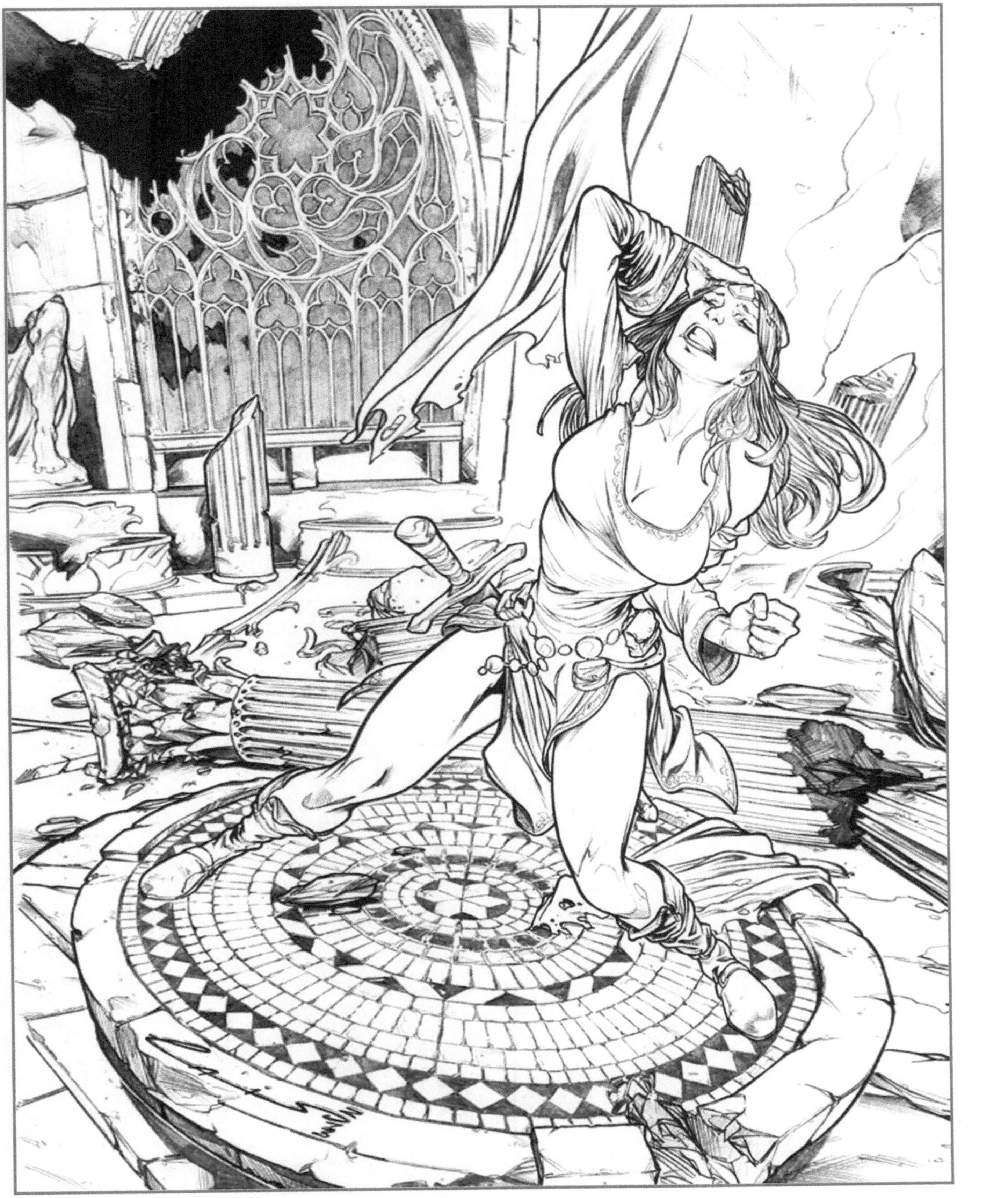

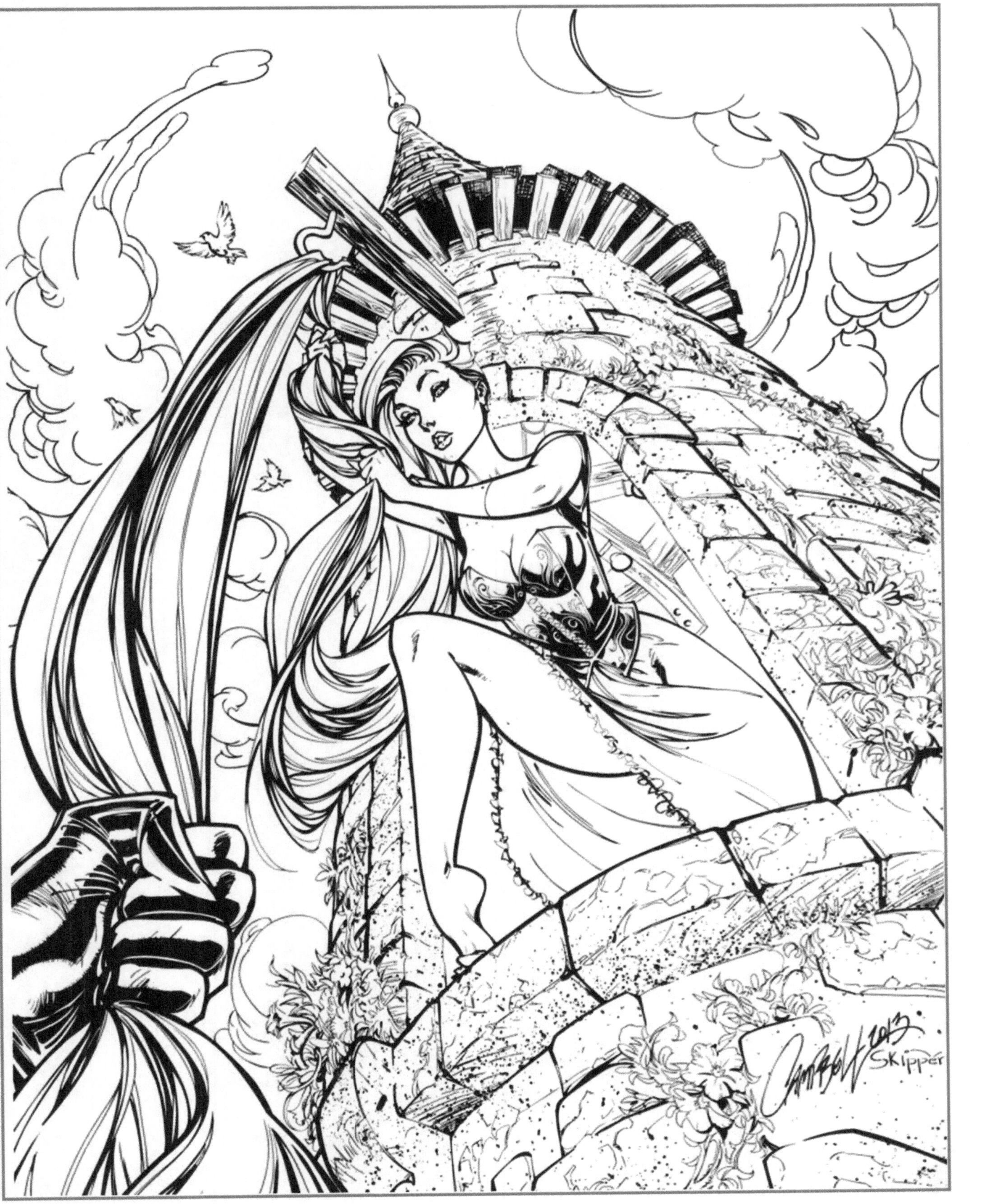
Skipper

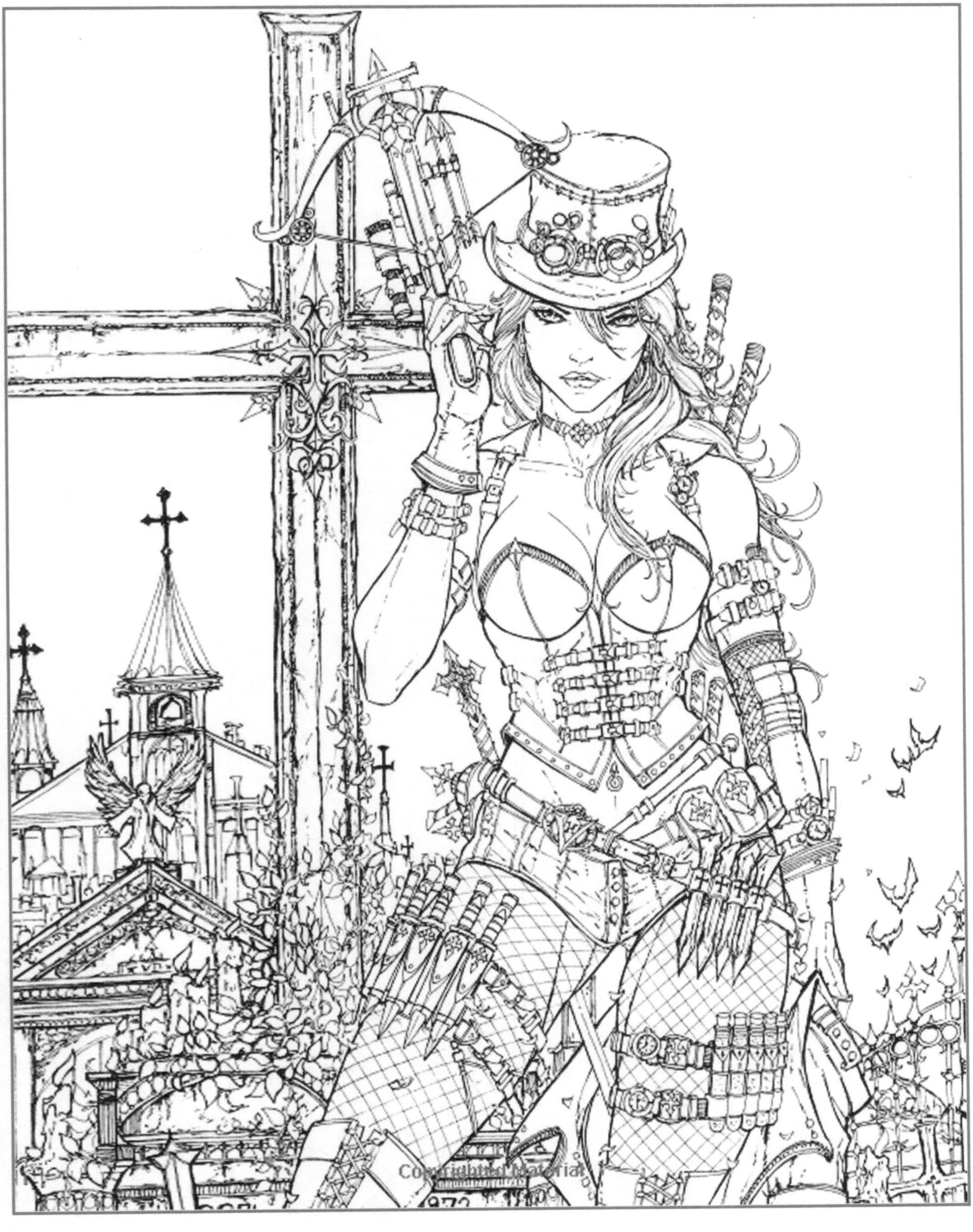

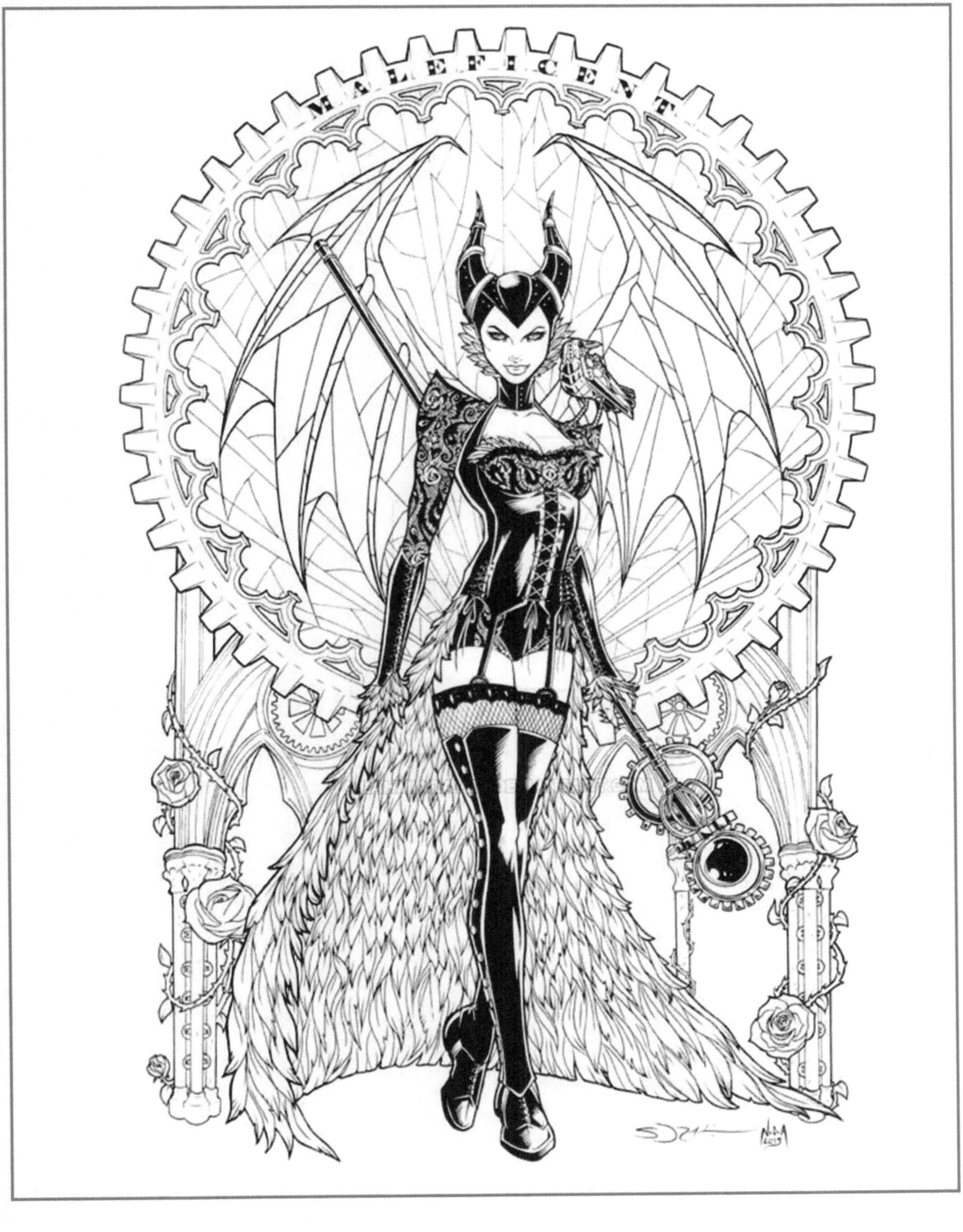
MALEFICENT

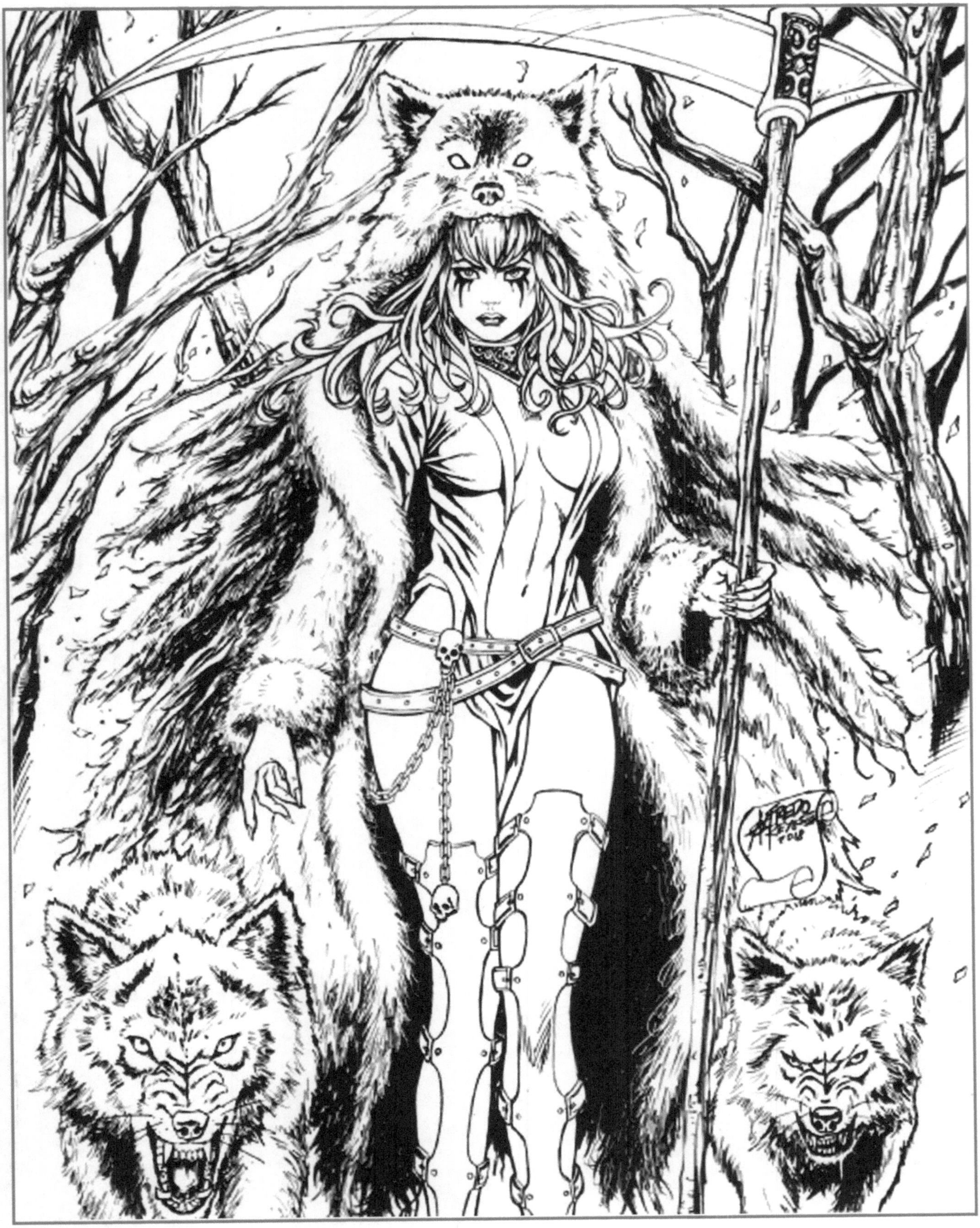

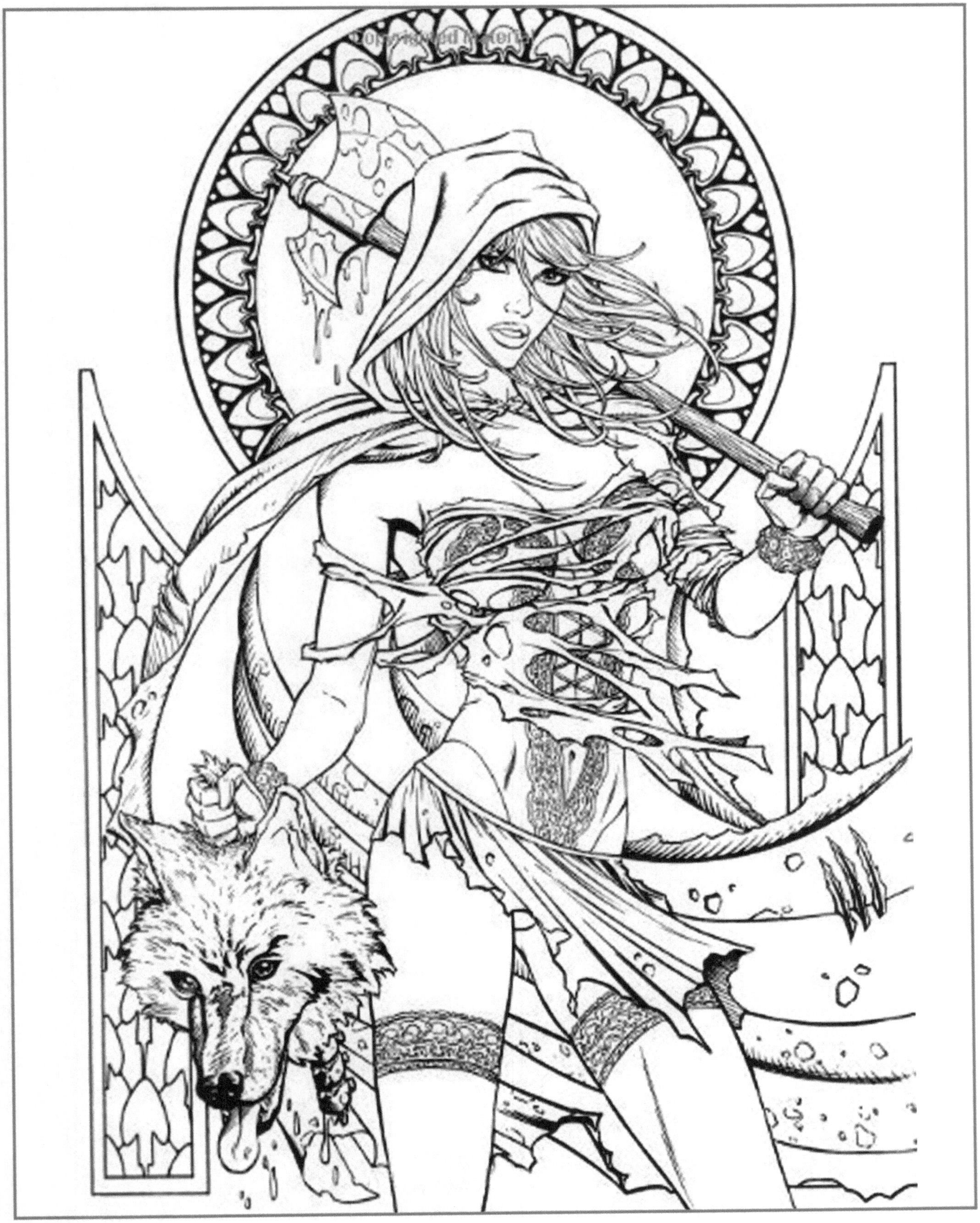

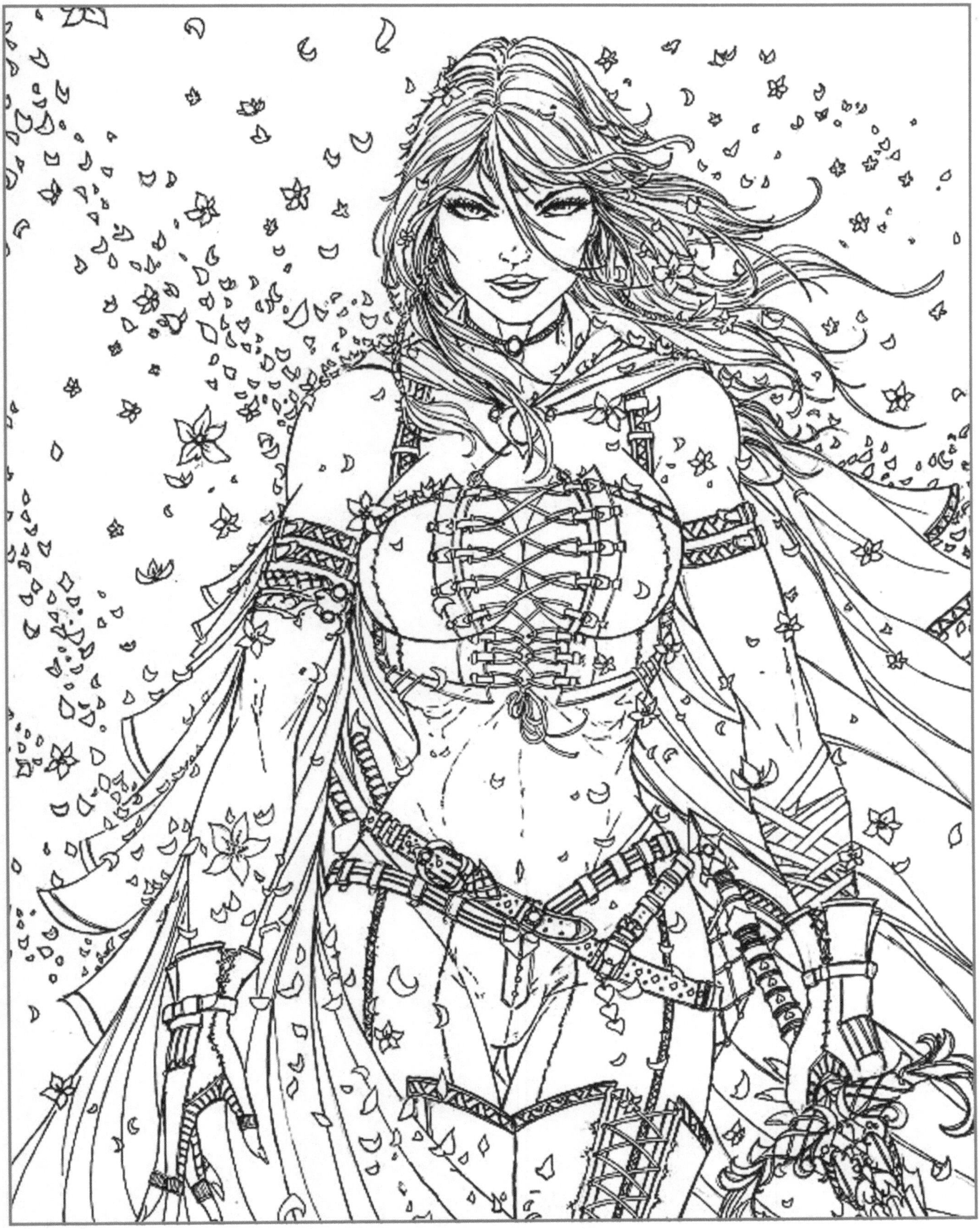

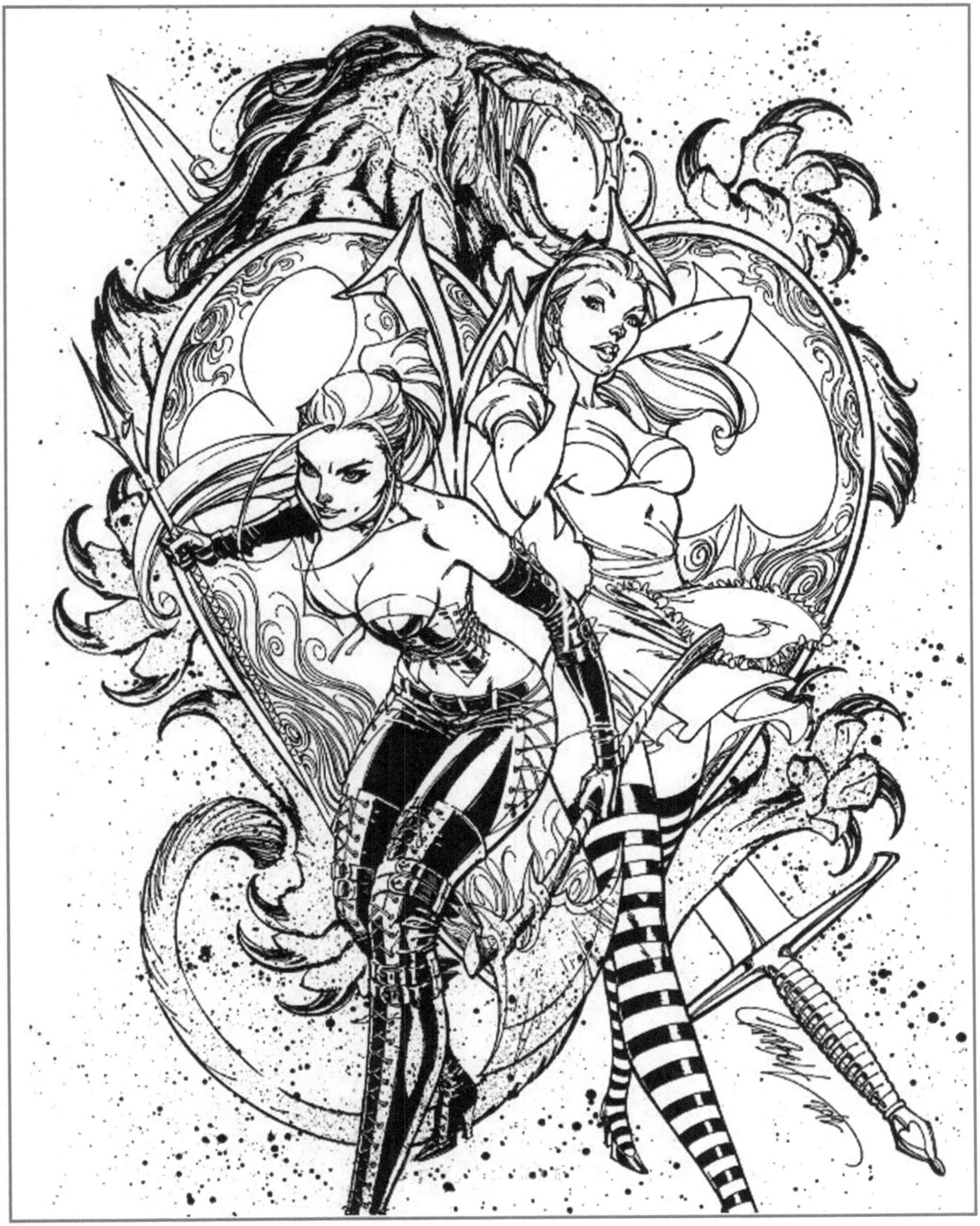

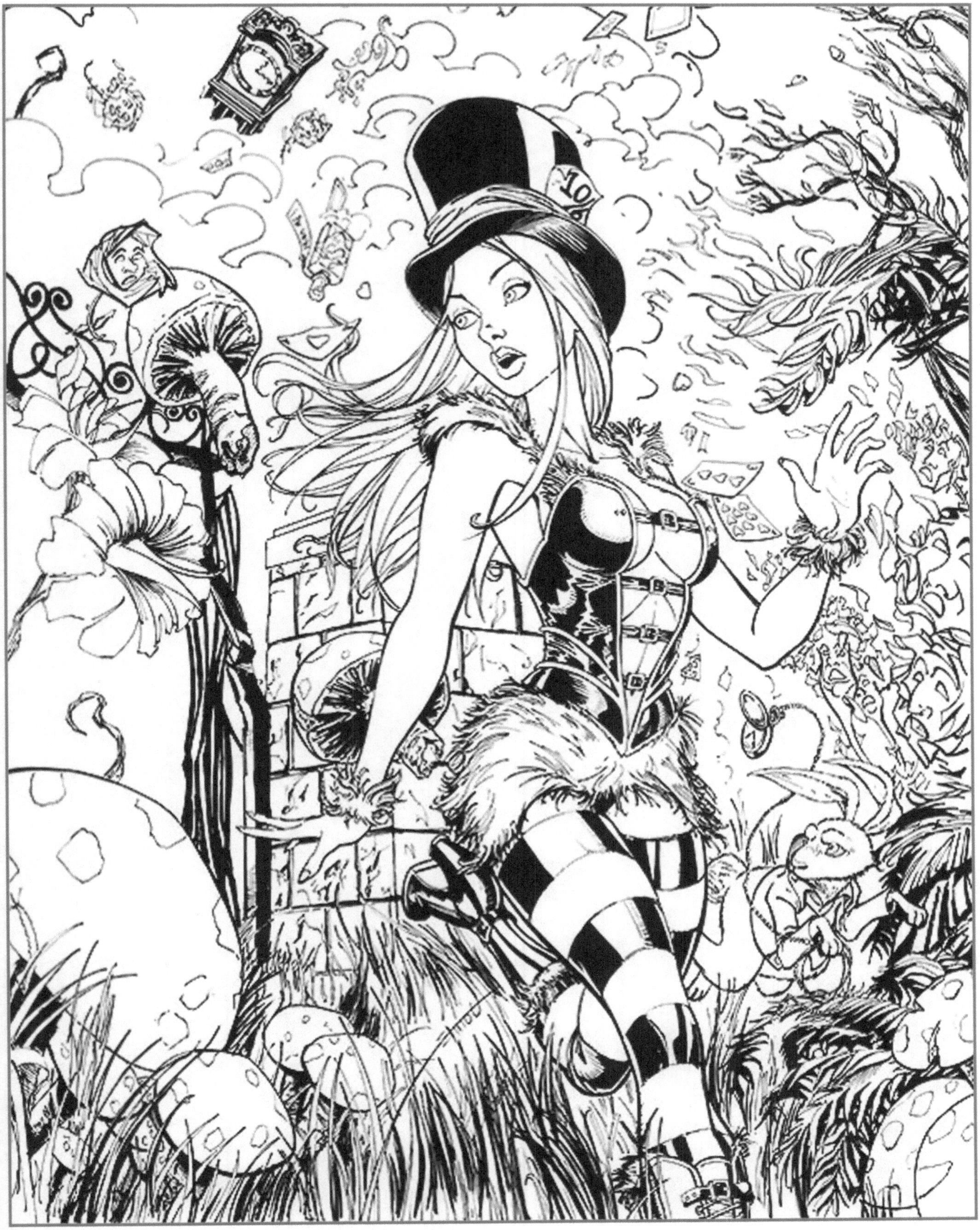

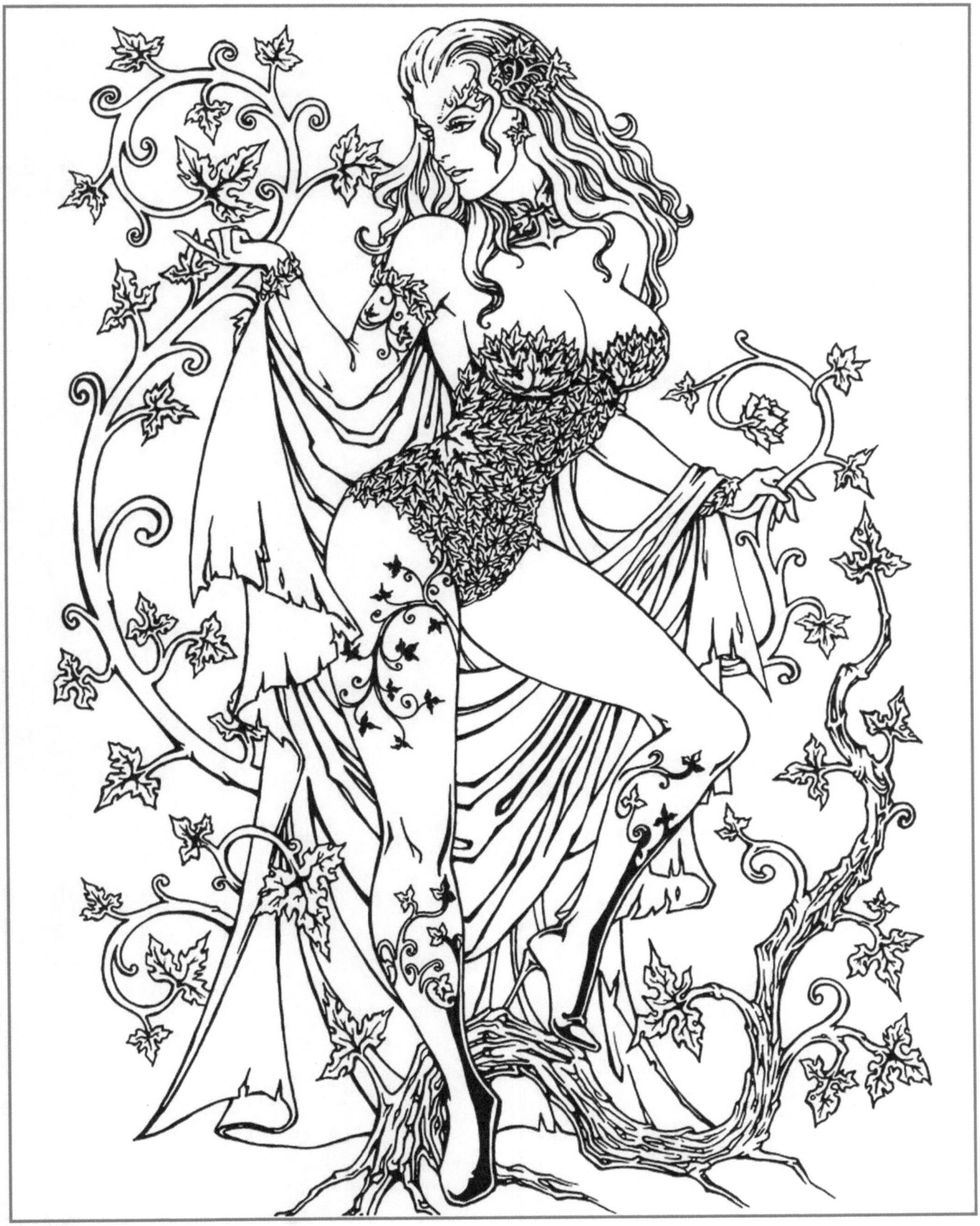

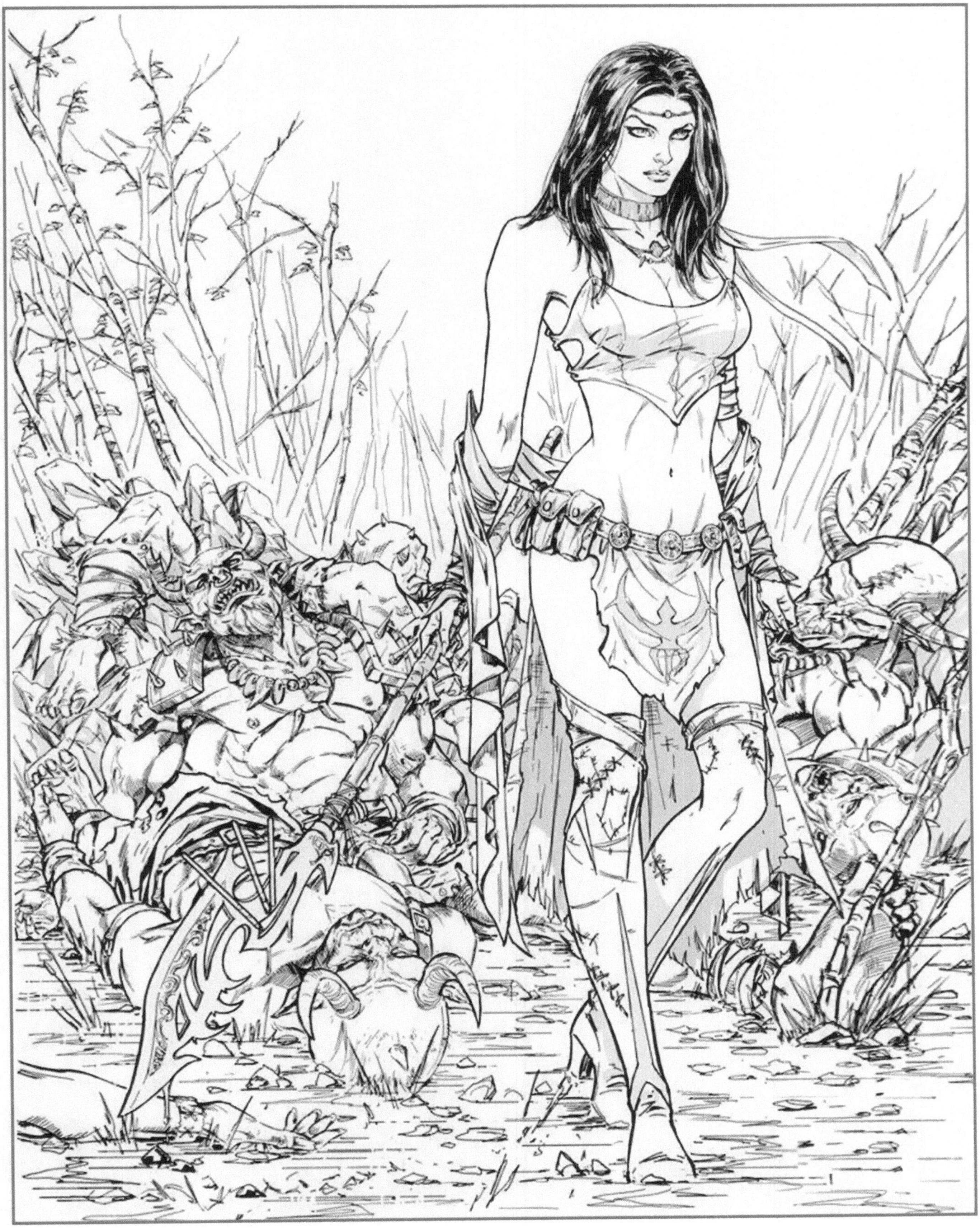

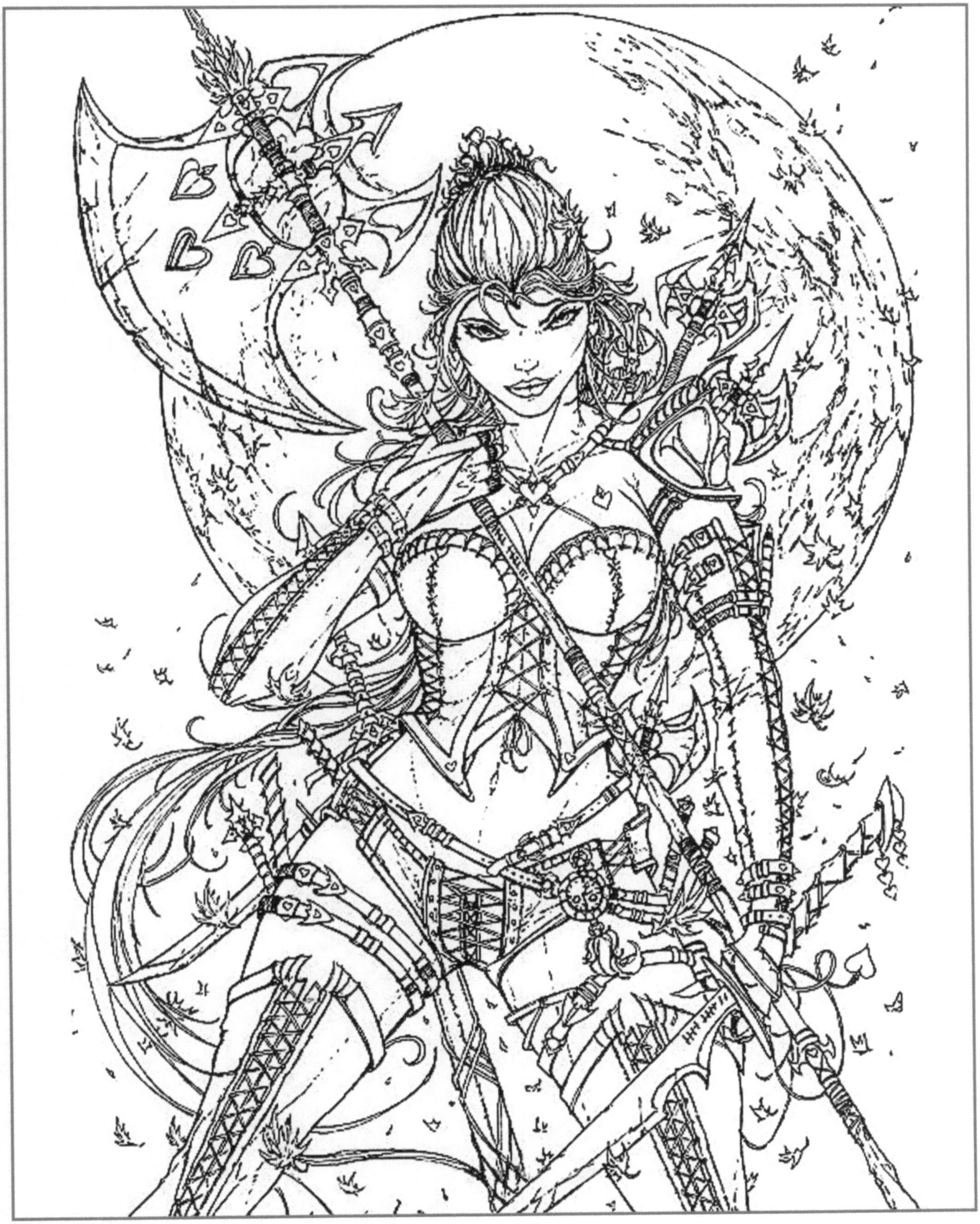

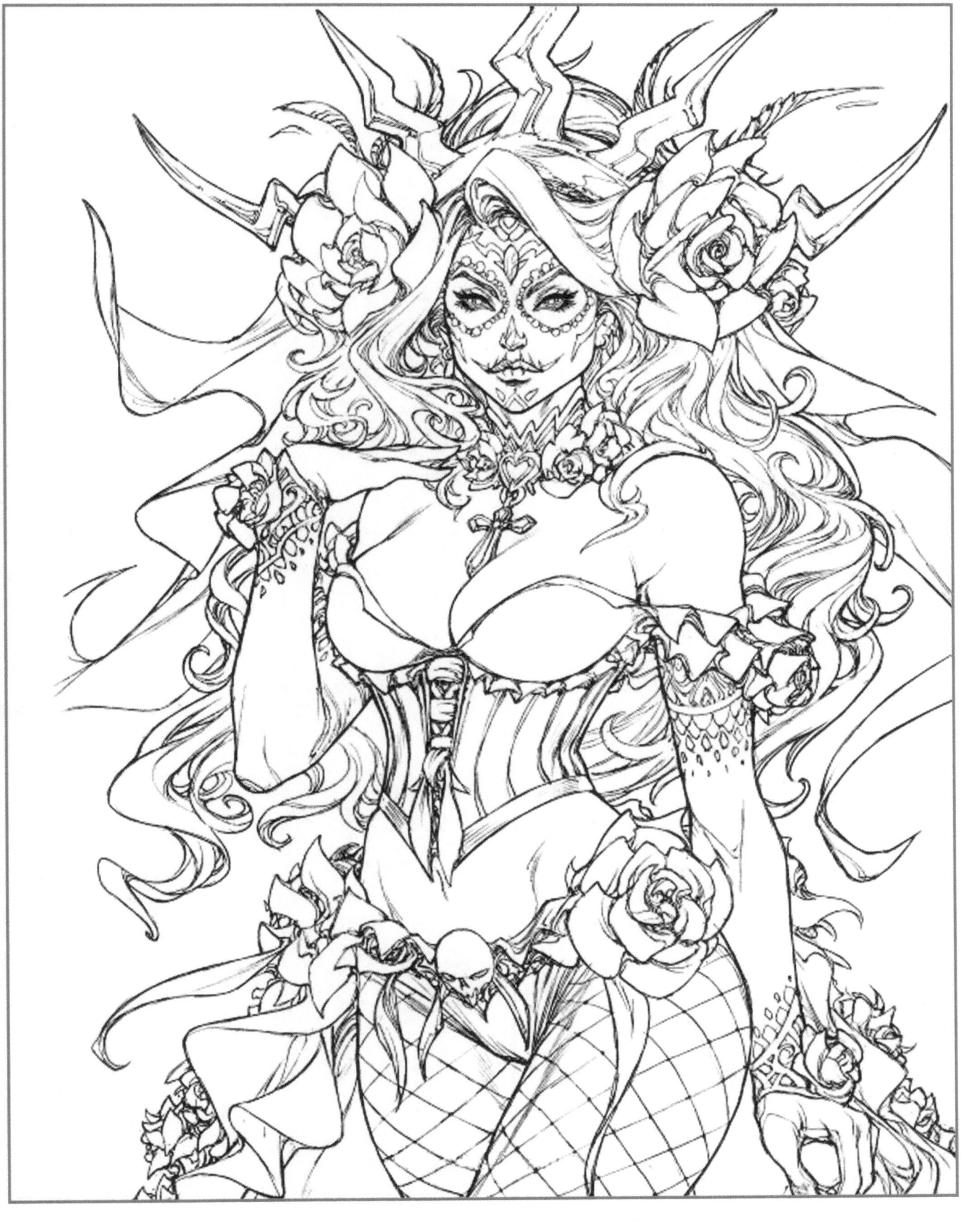

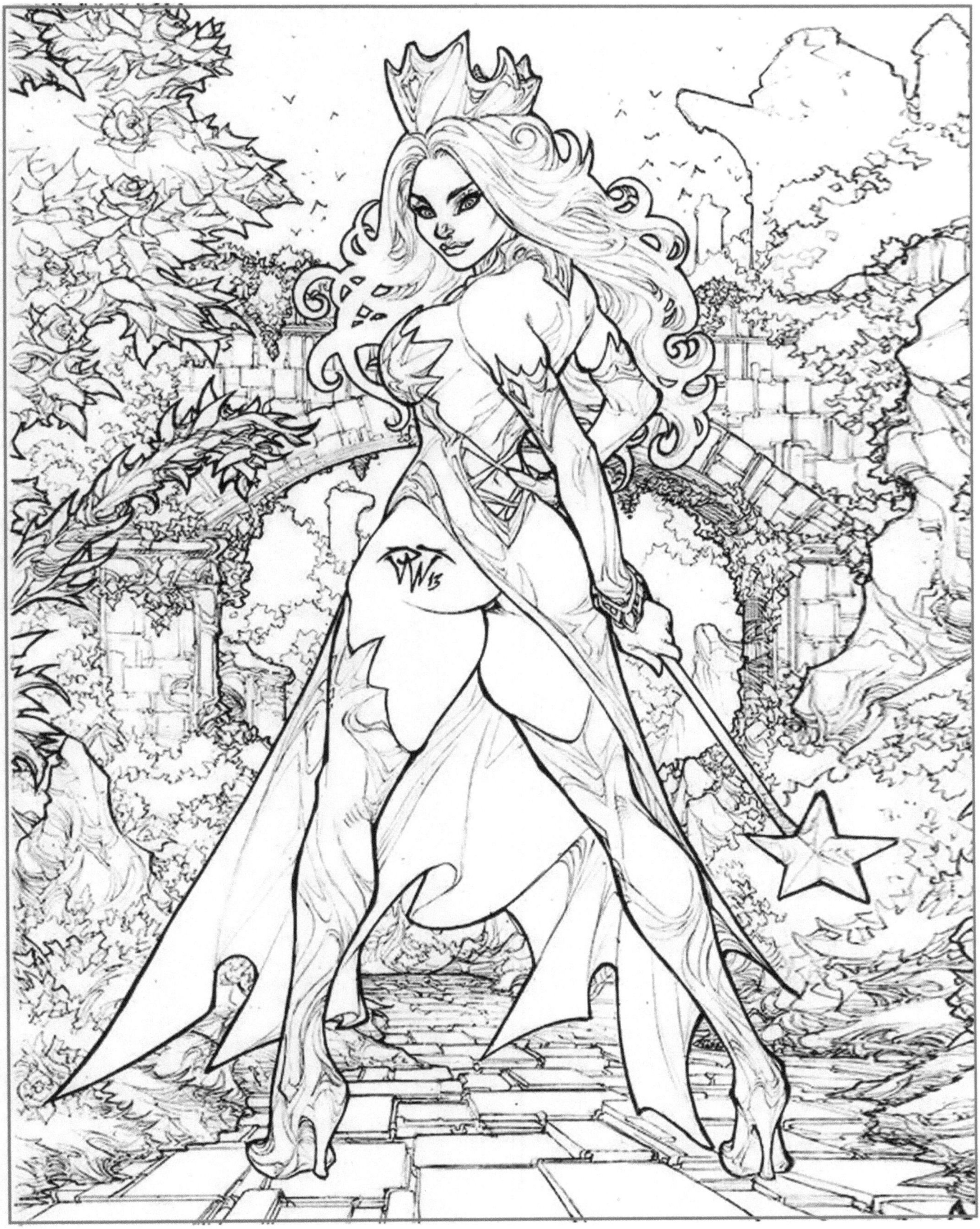

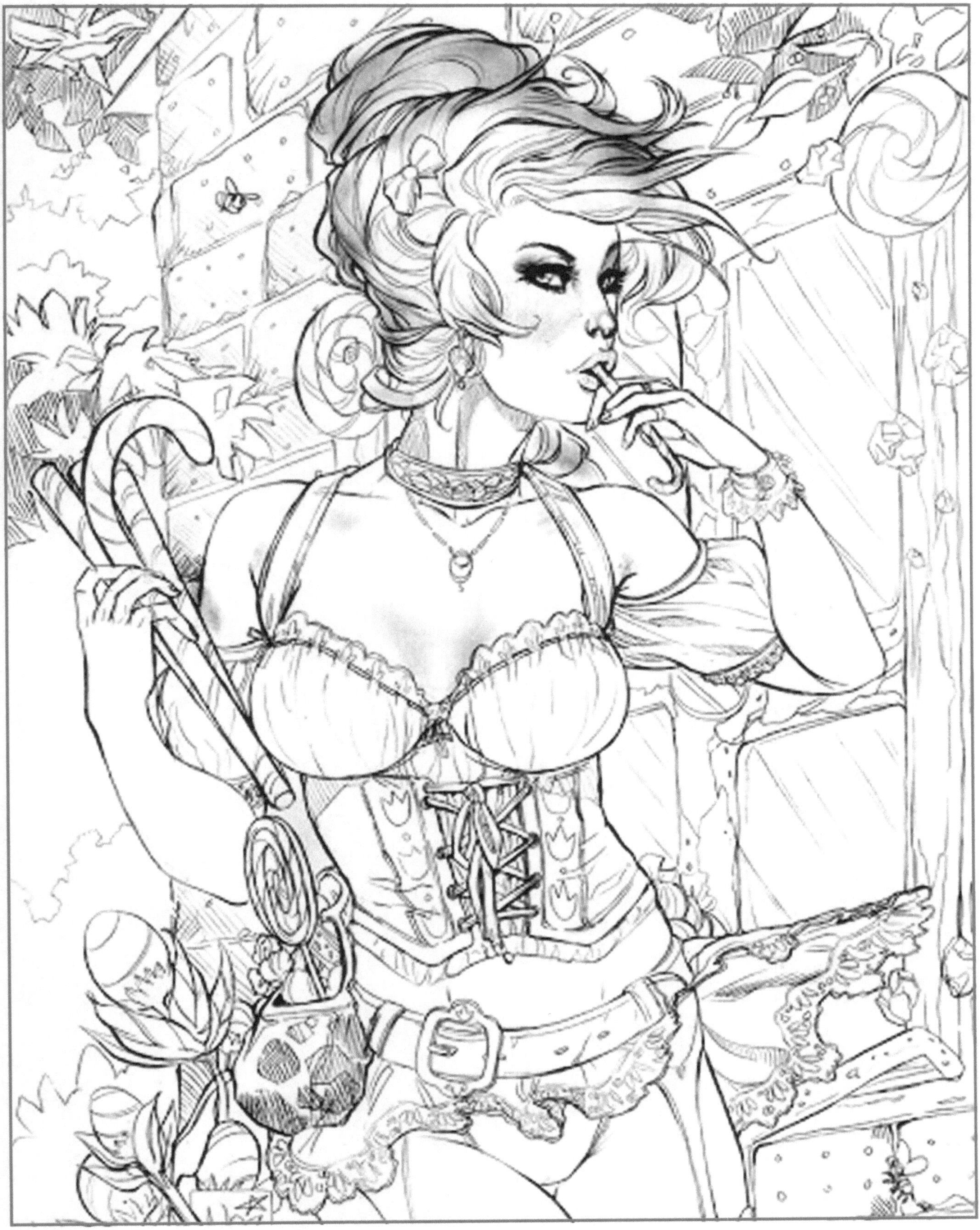

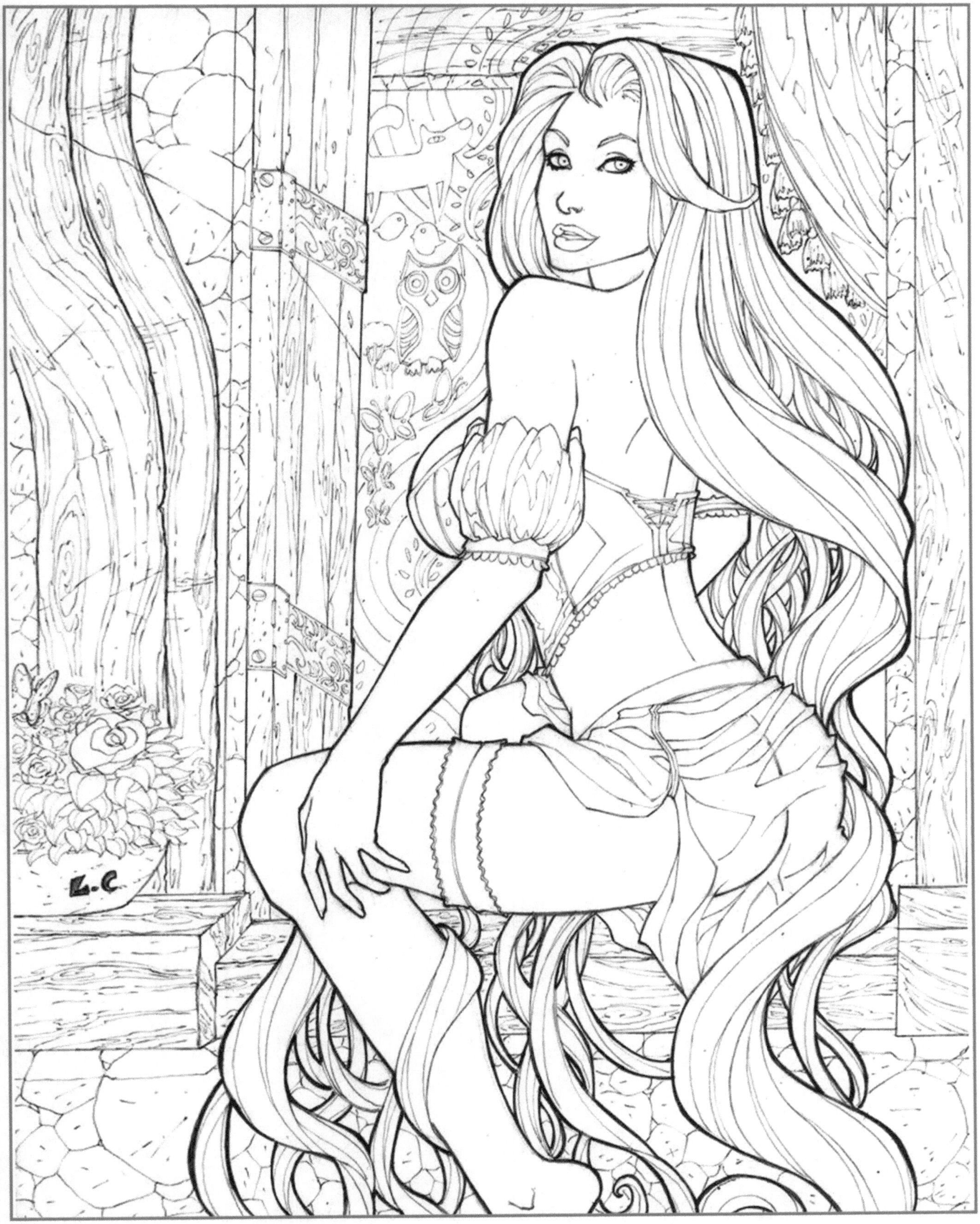
L.C

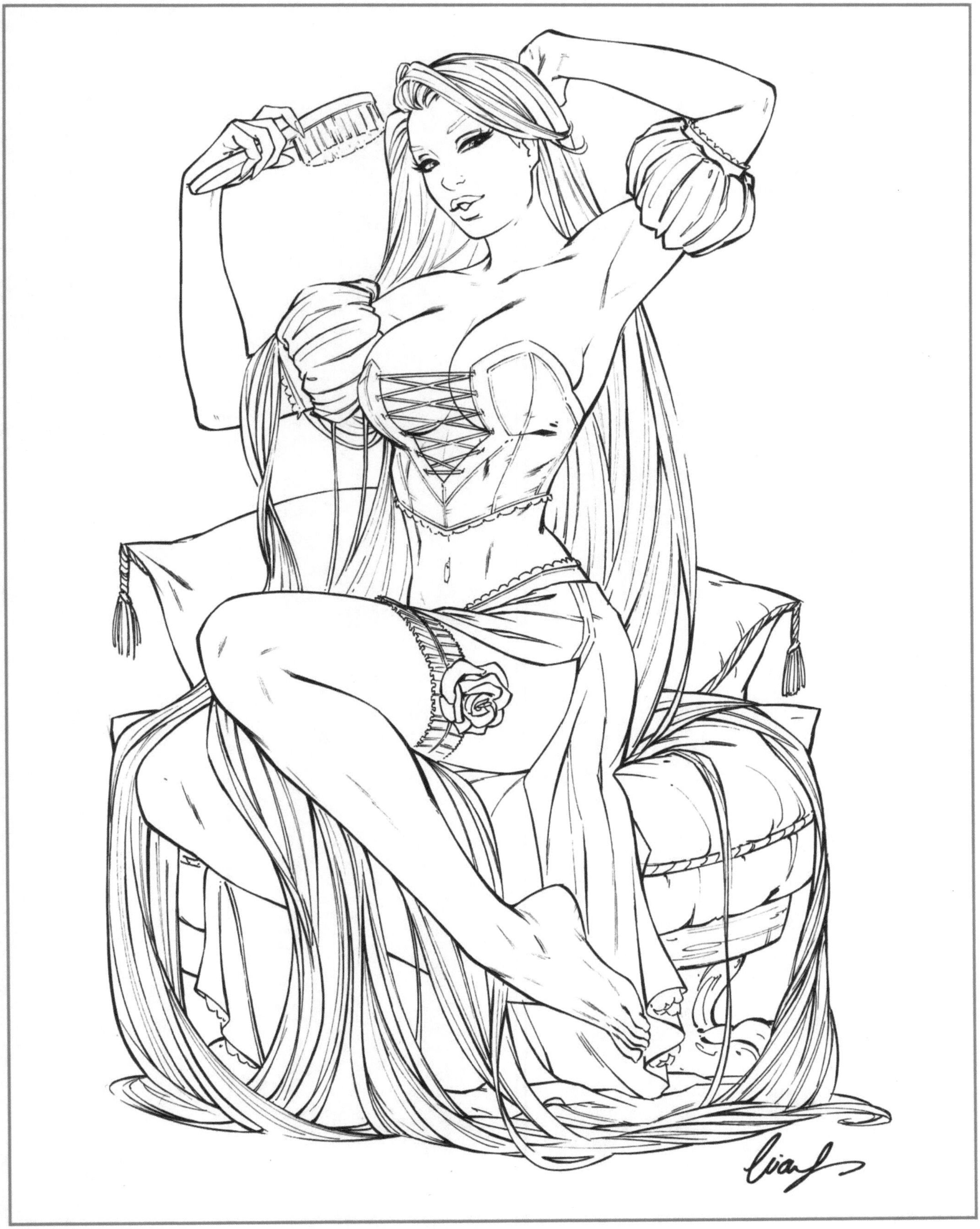

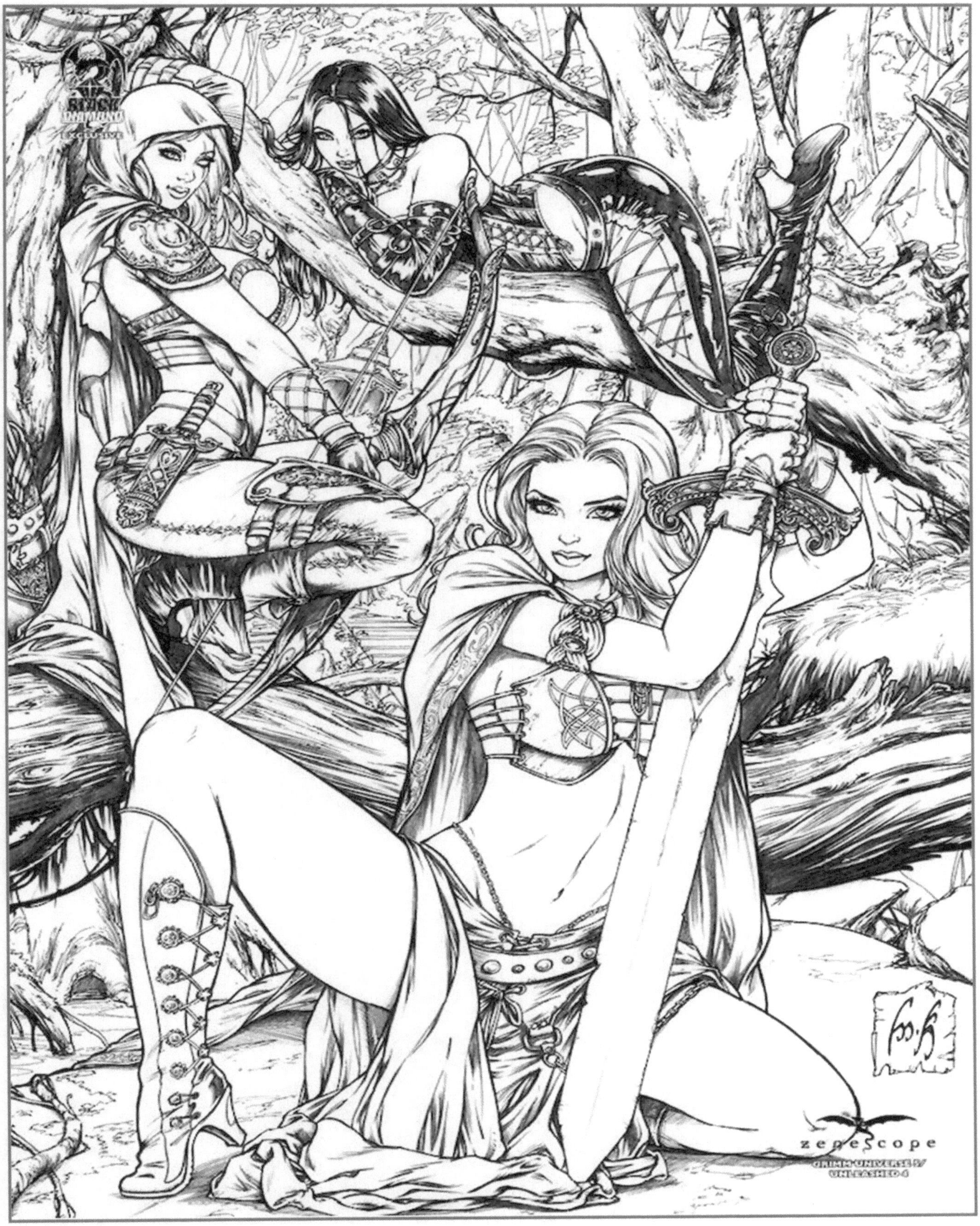
zenescope
GRIMM UNIVERSE 5/
UNLEASHED 4

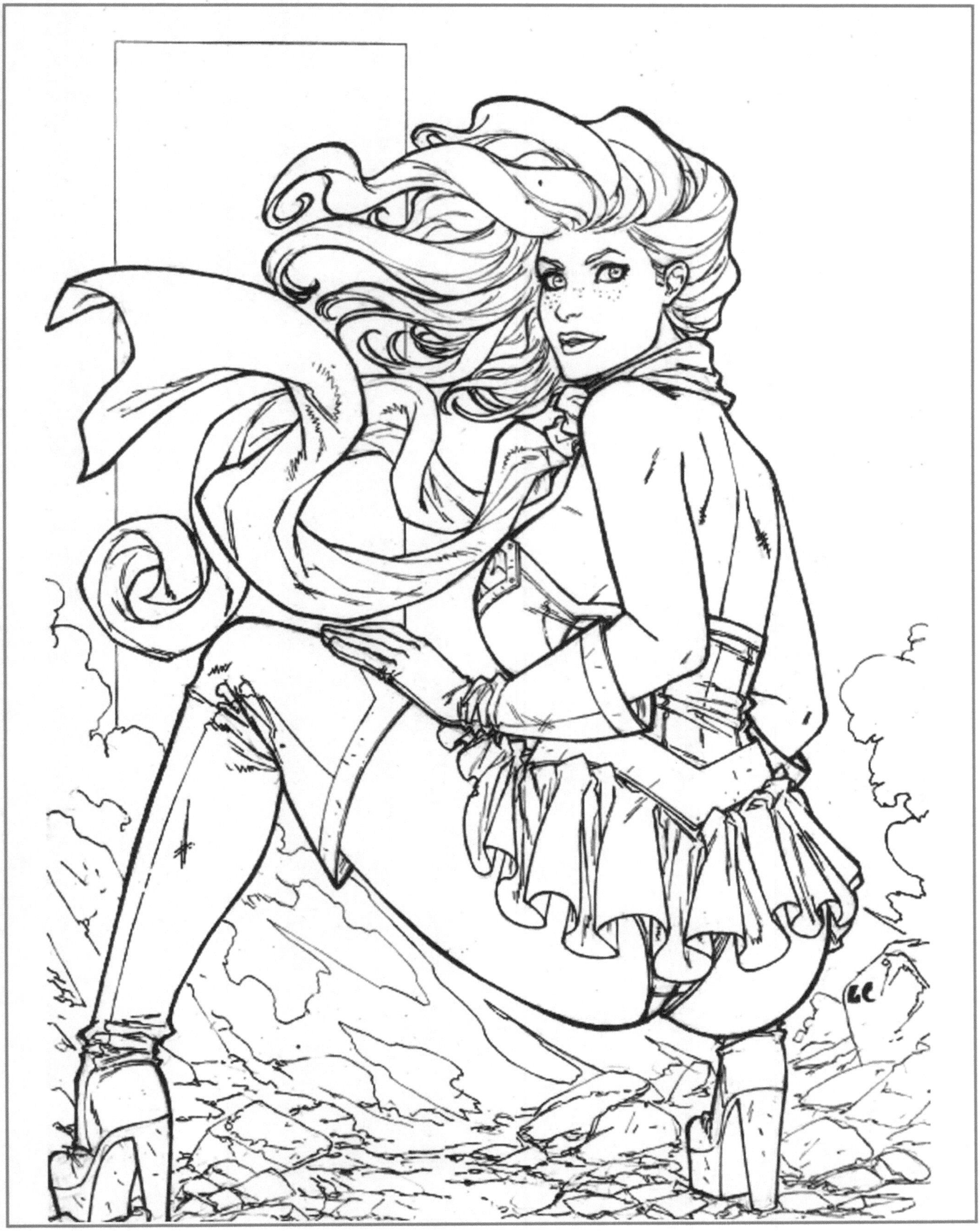

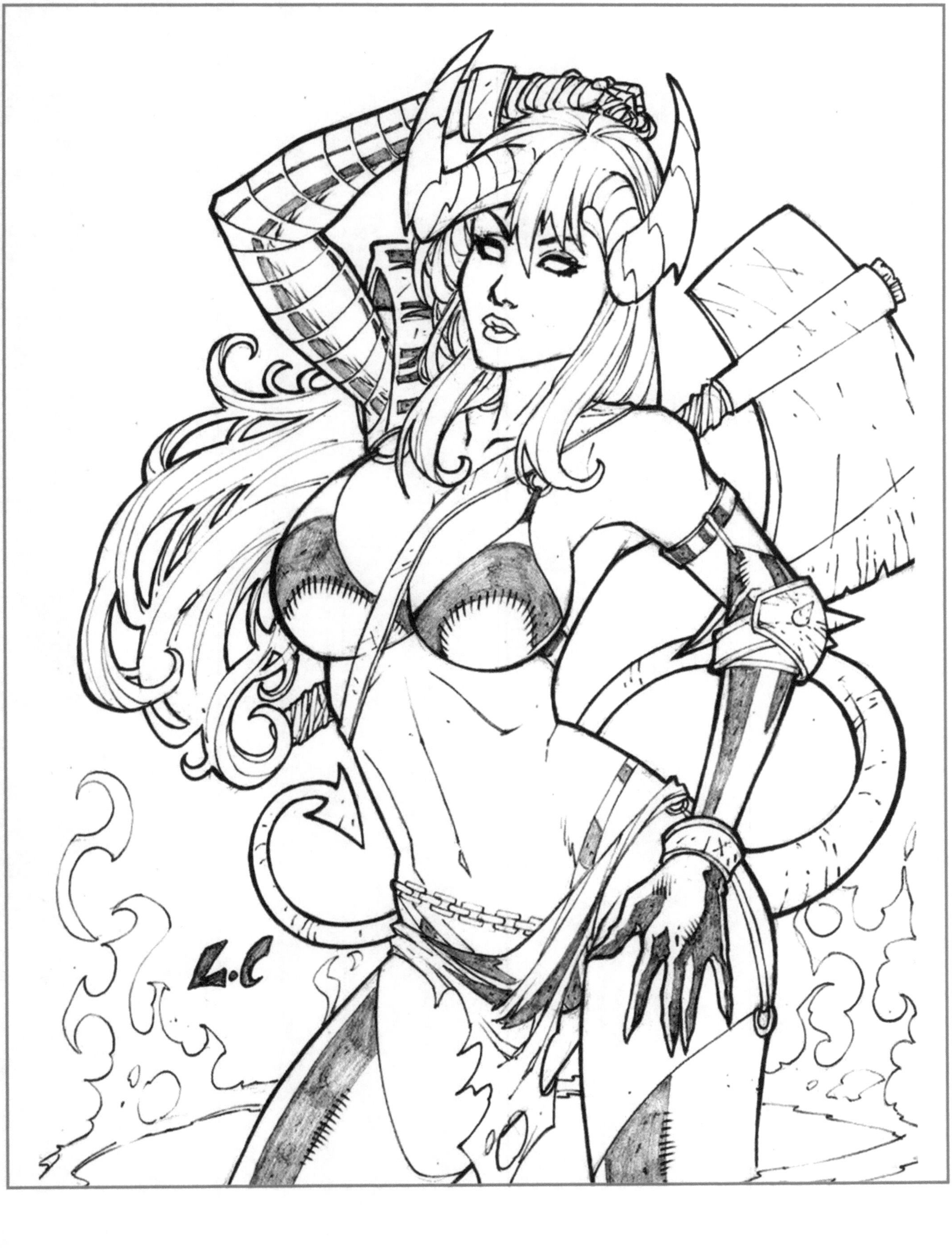

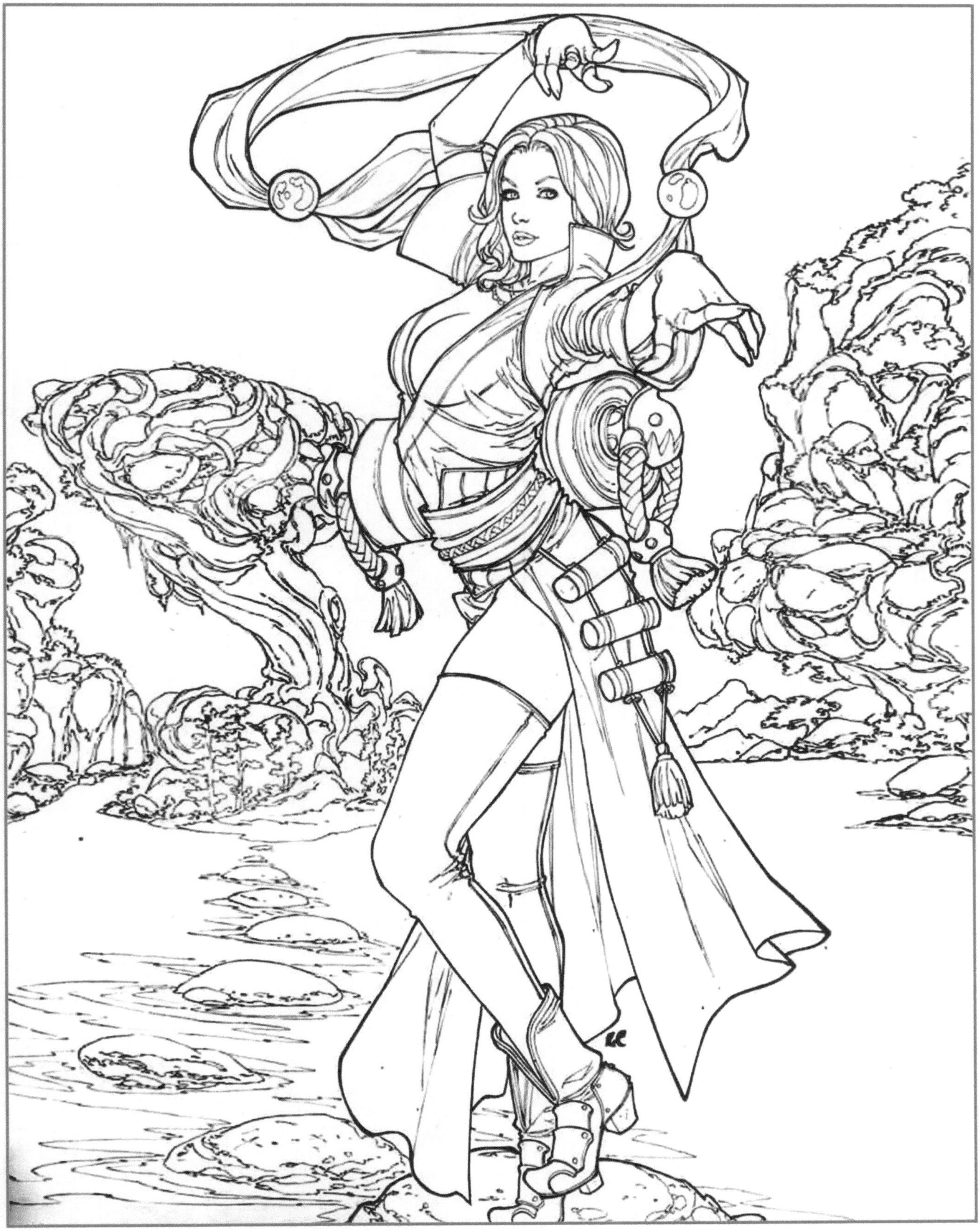

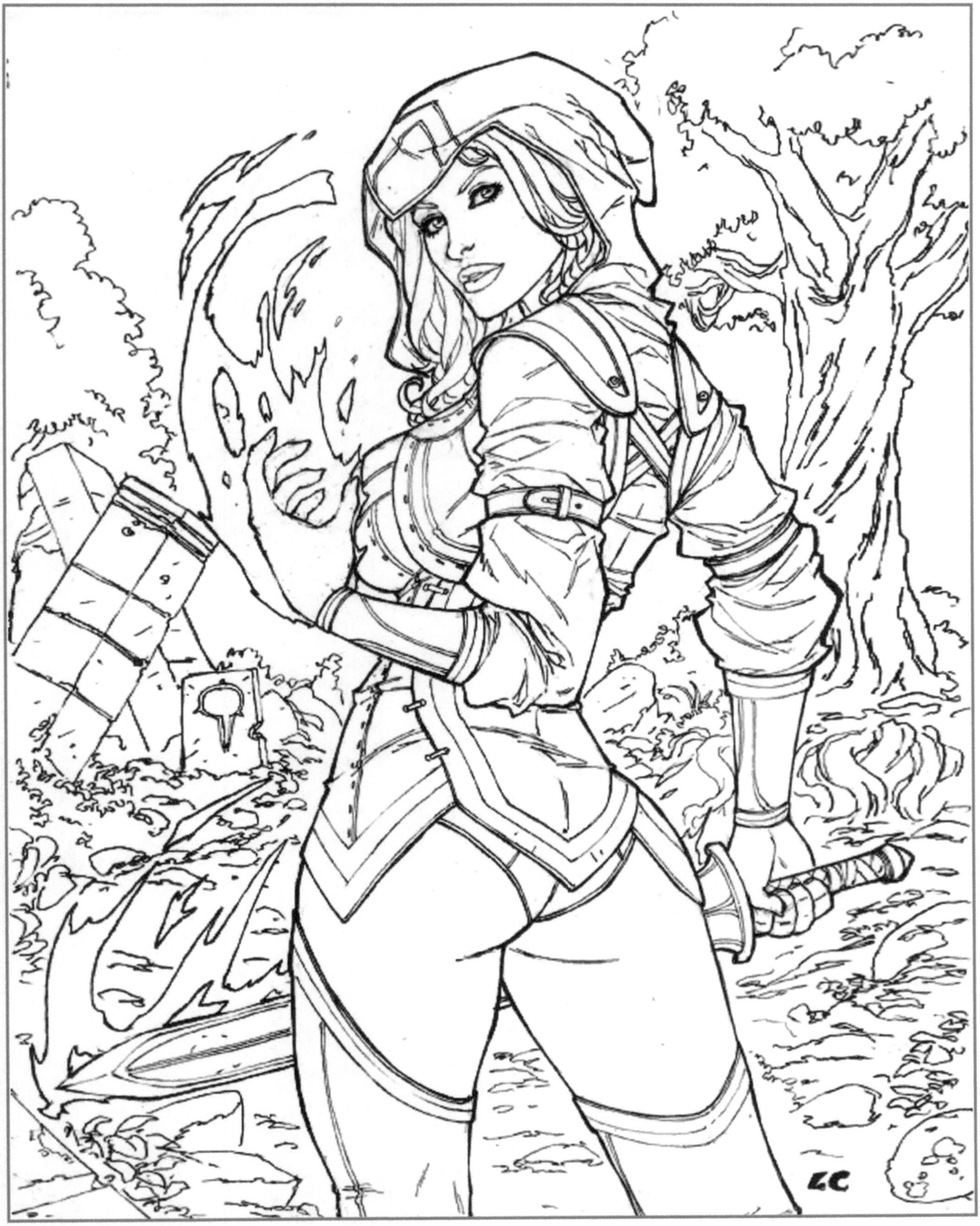
LC

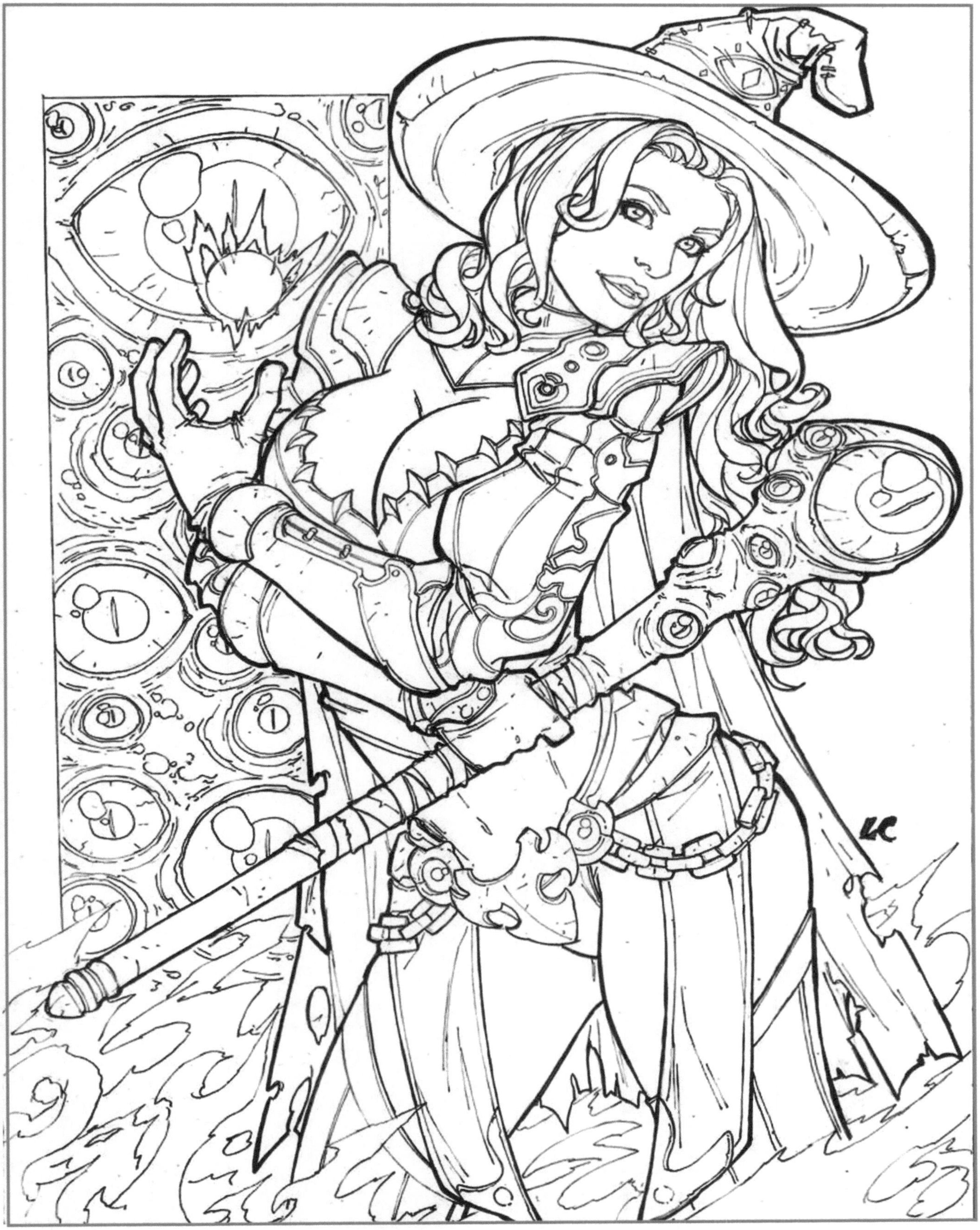
LC

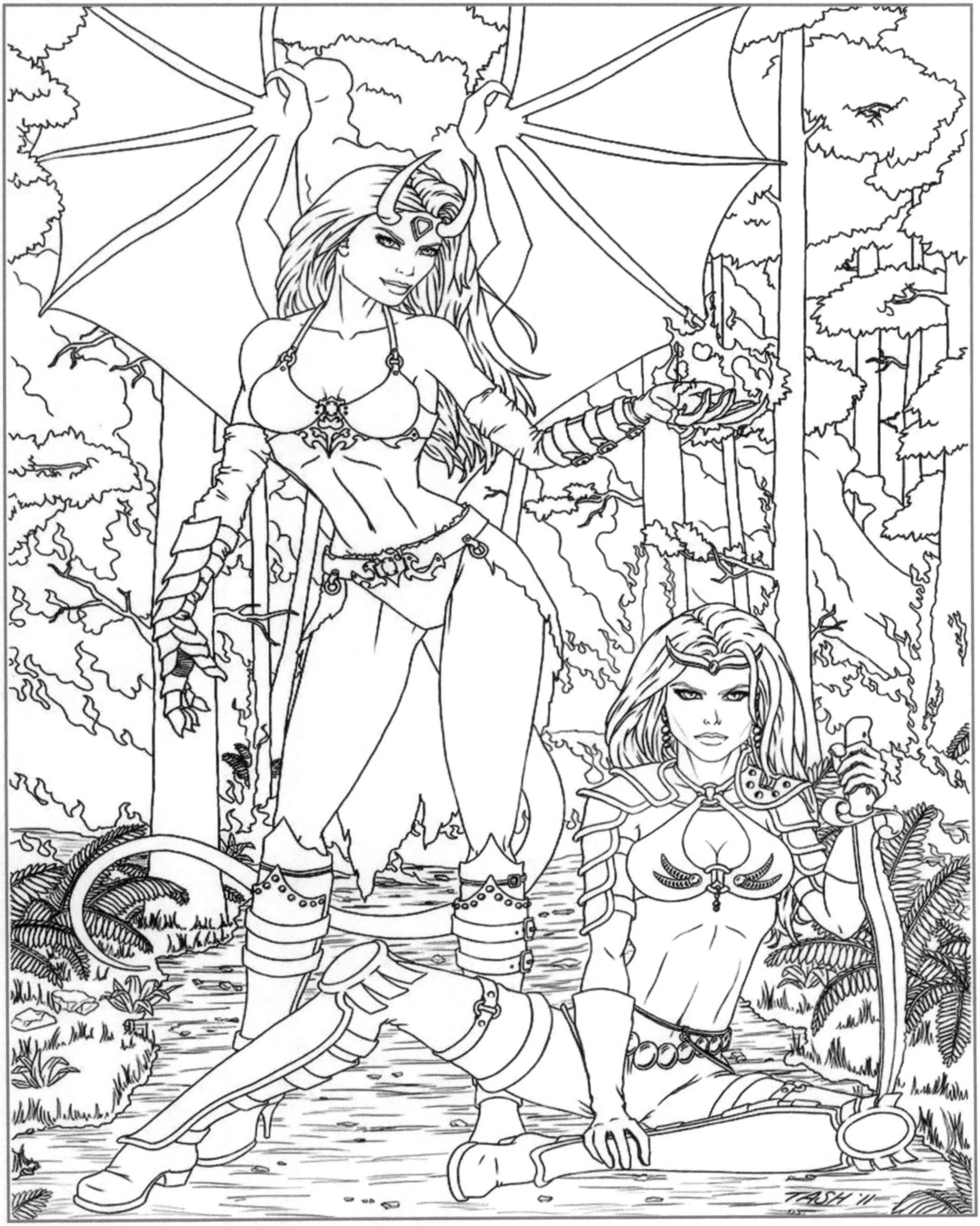
TASH '11

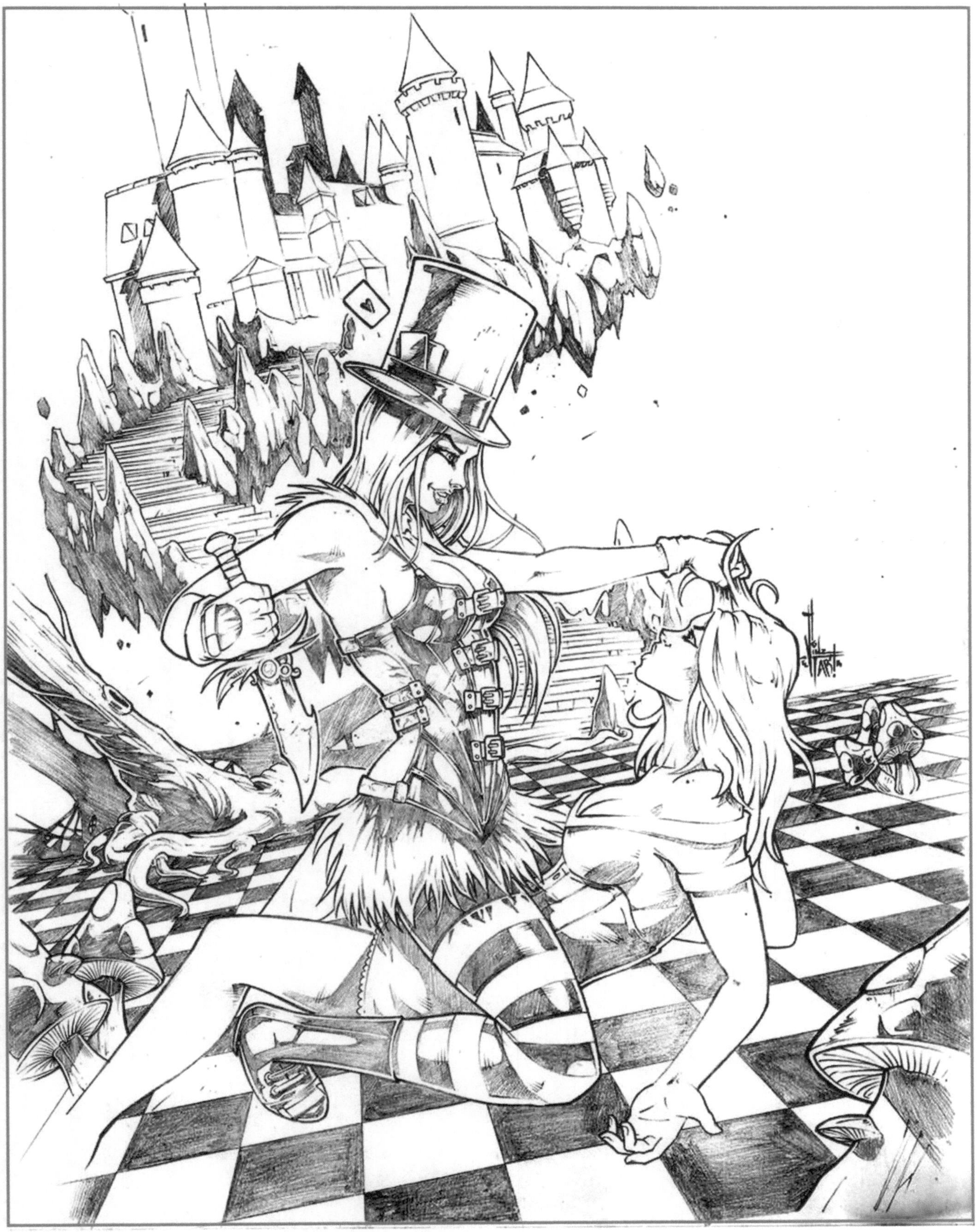

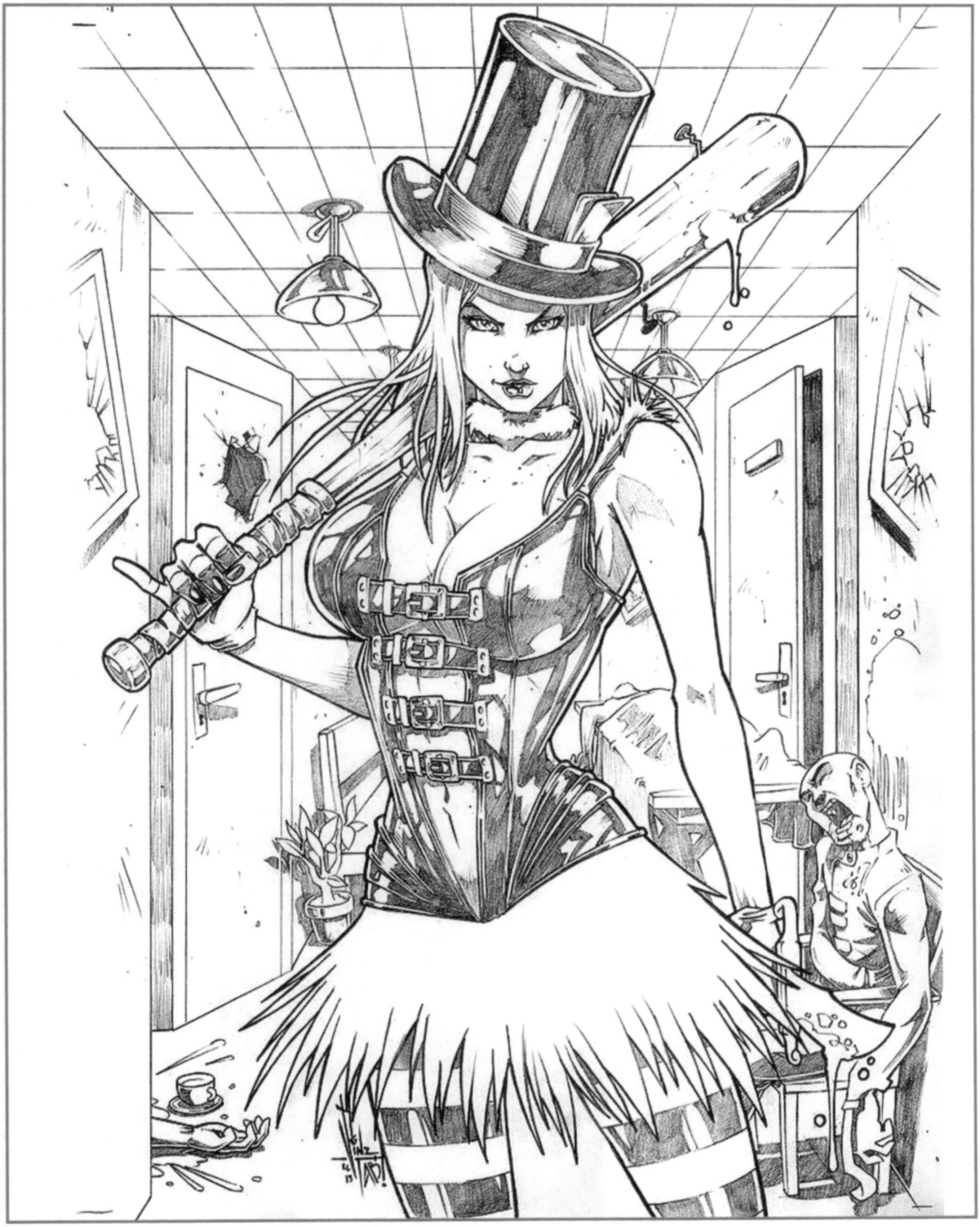

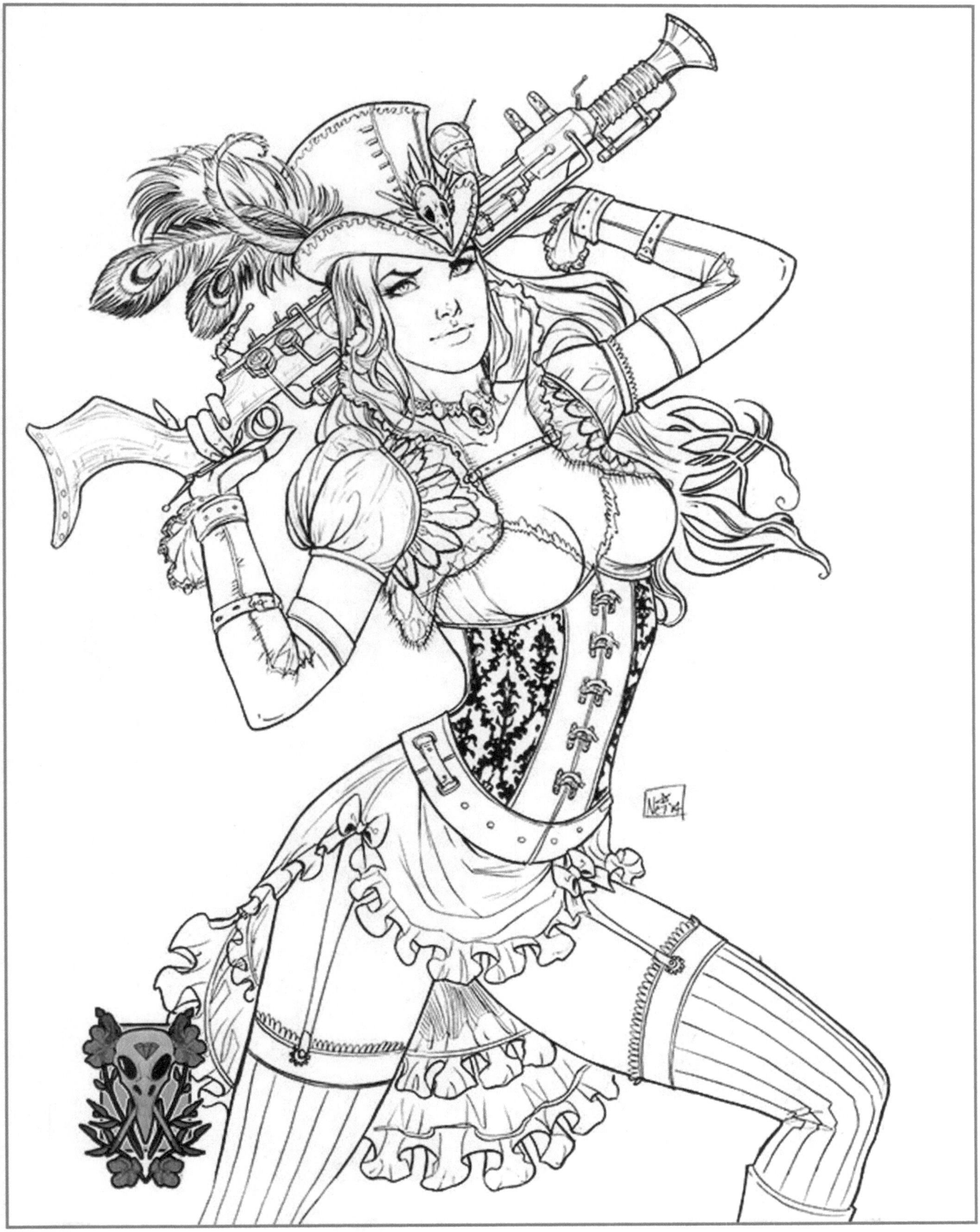

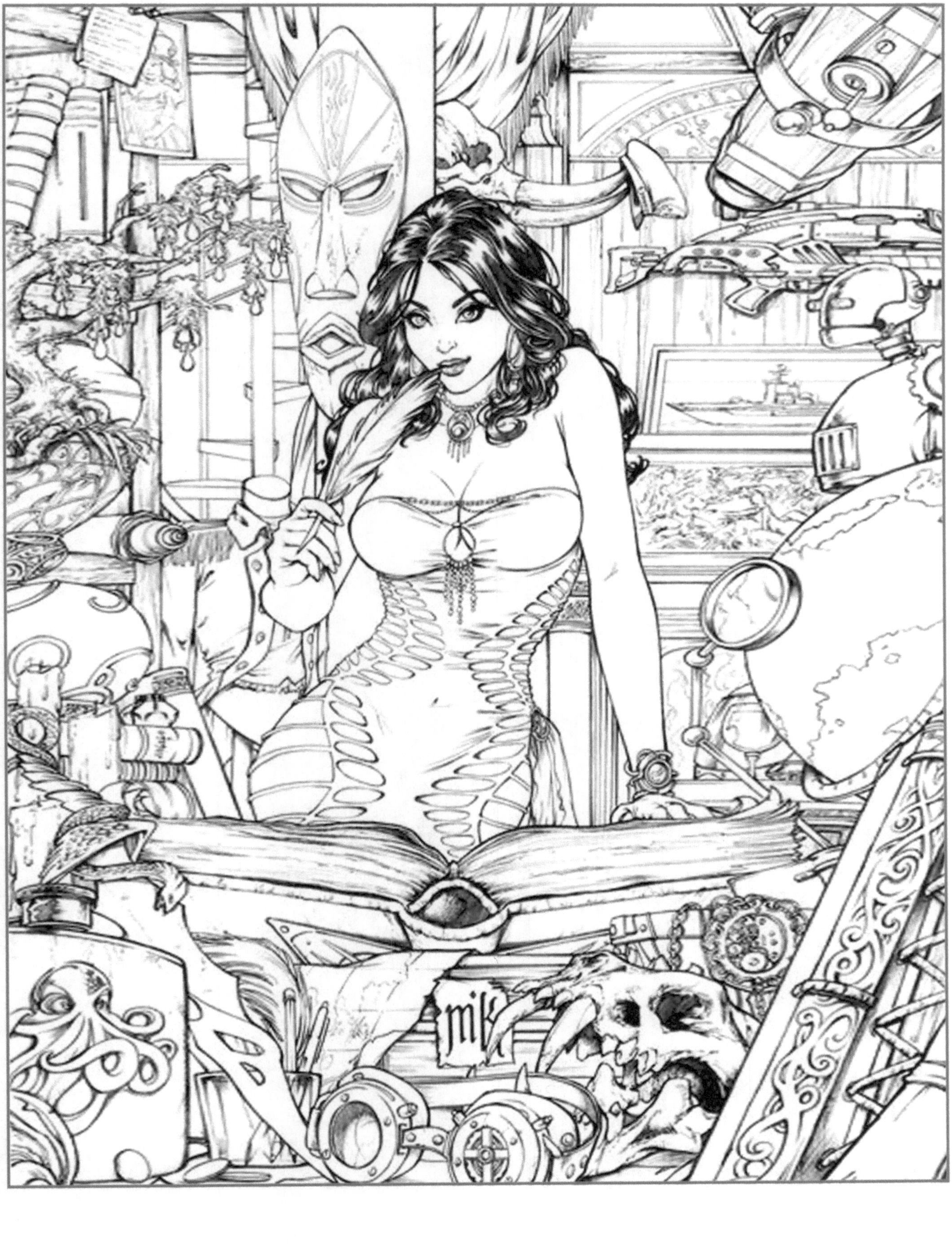

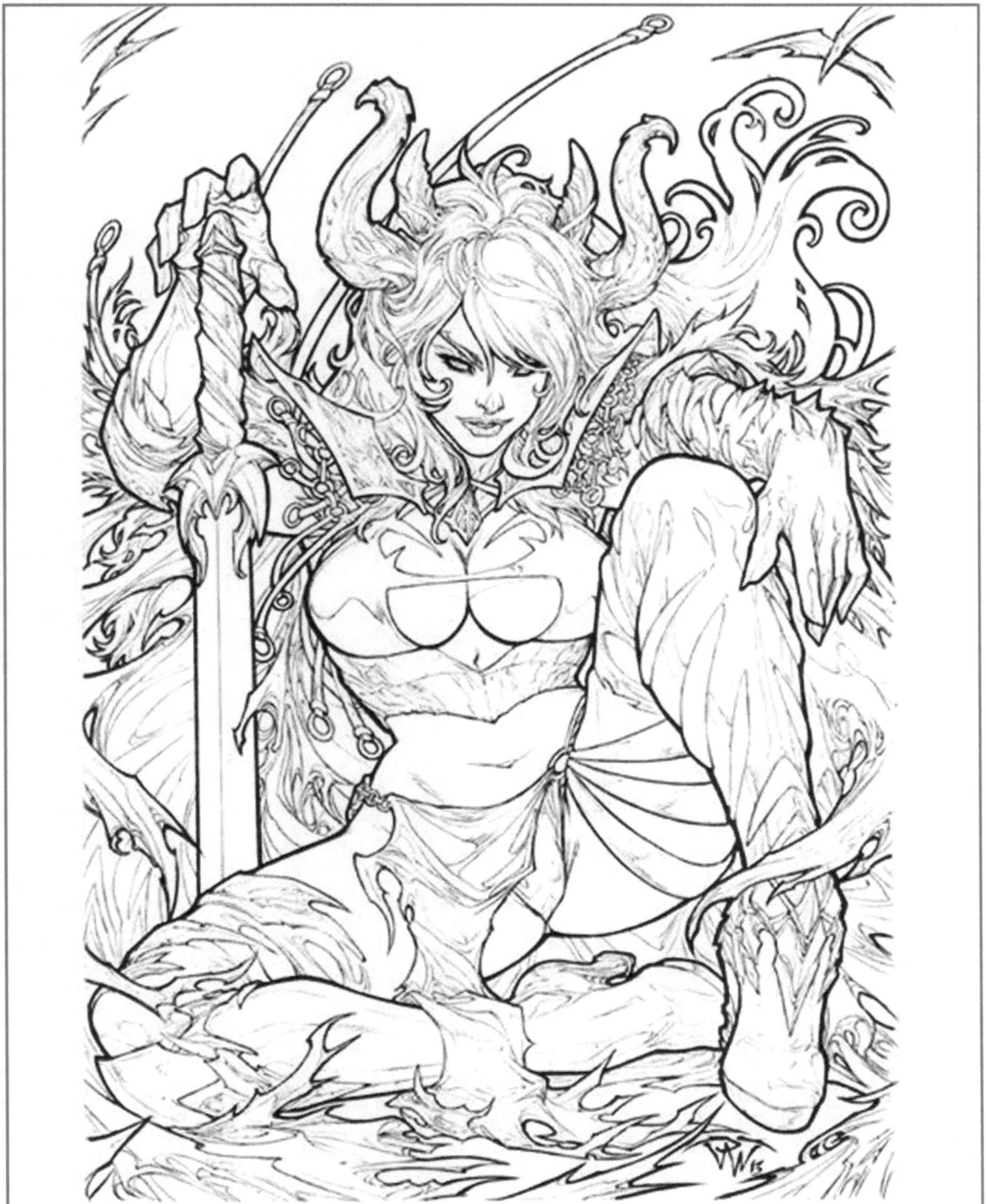

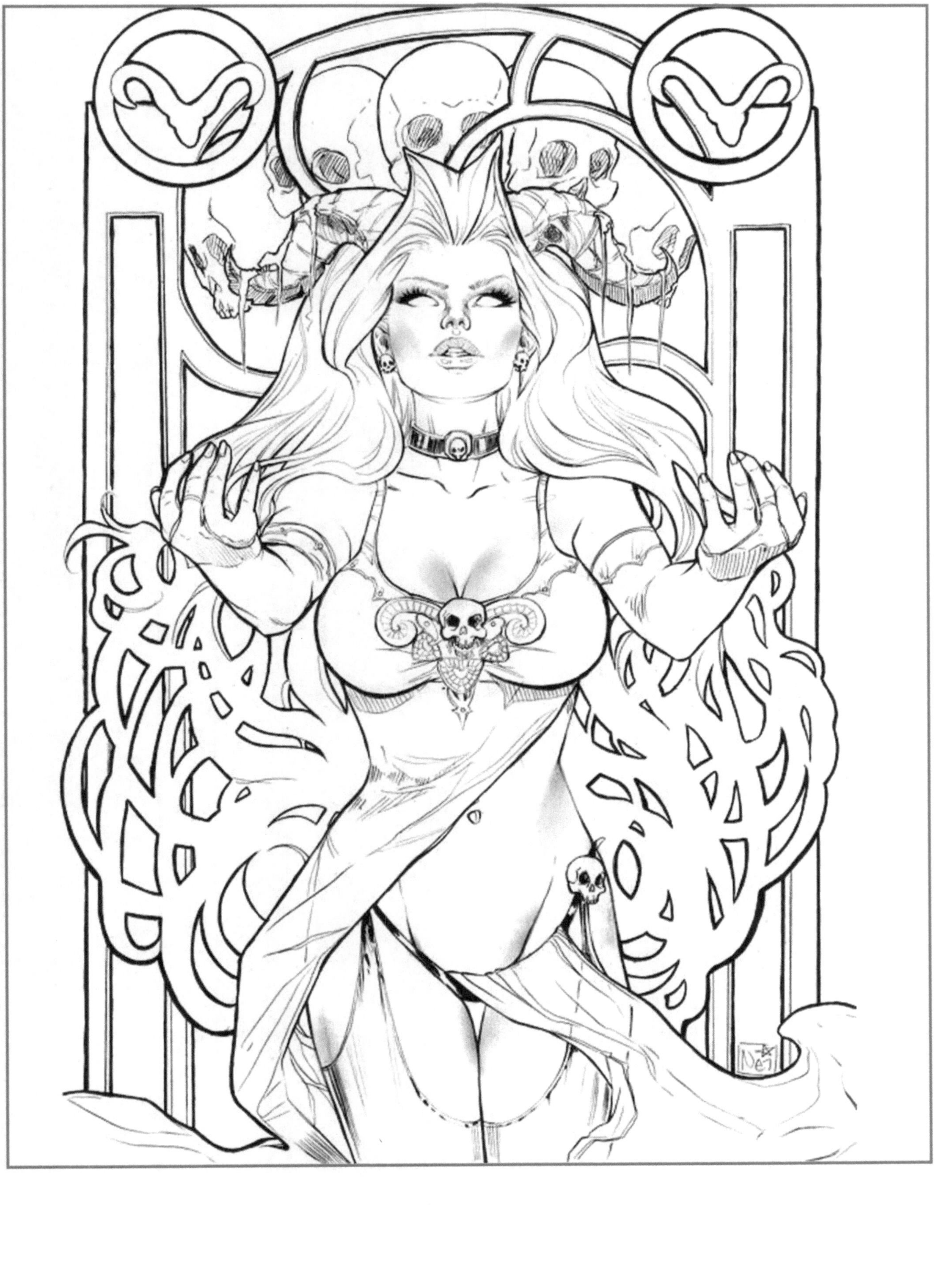

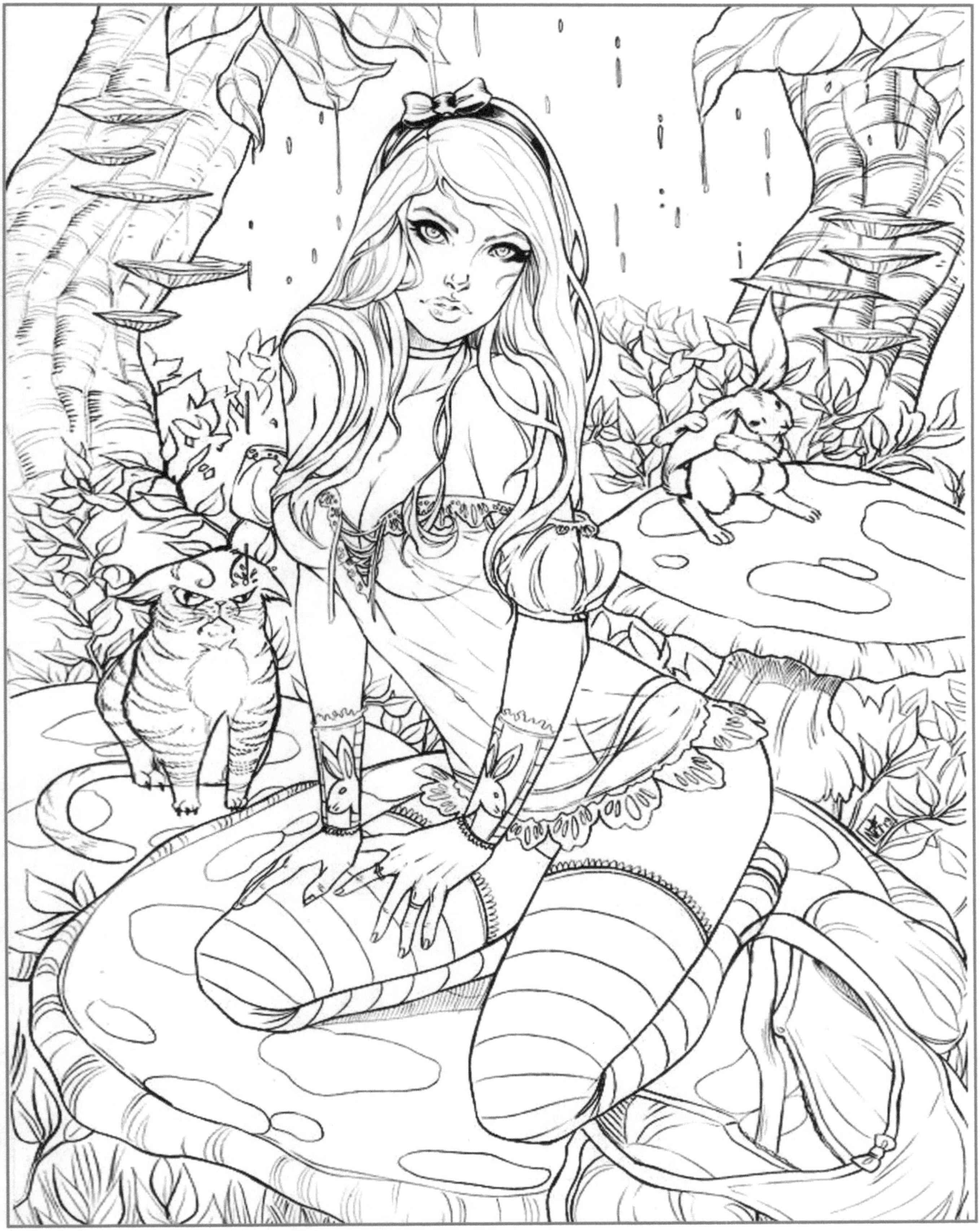

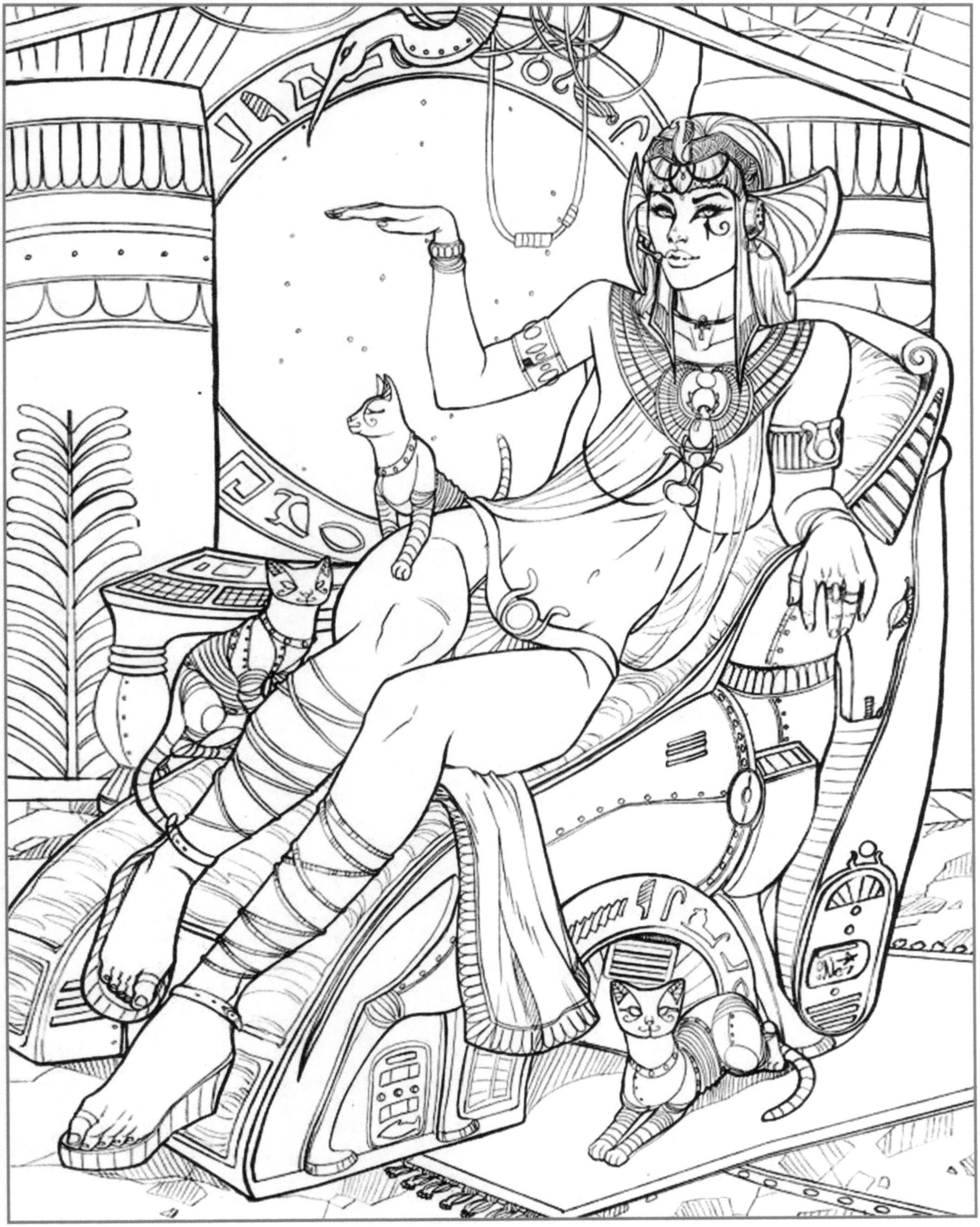

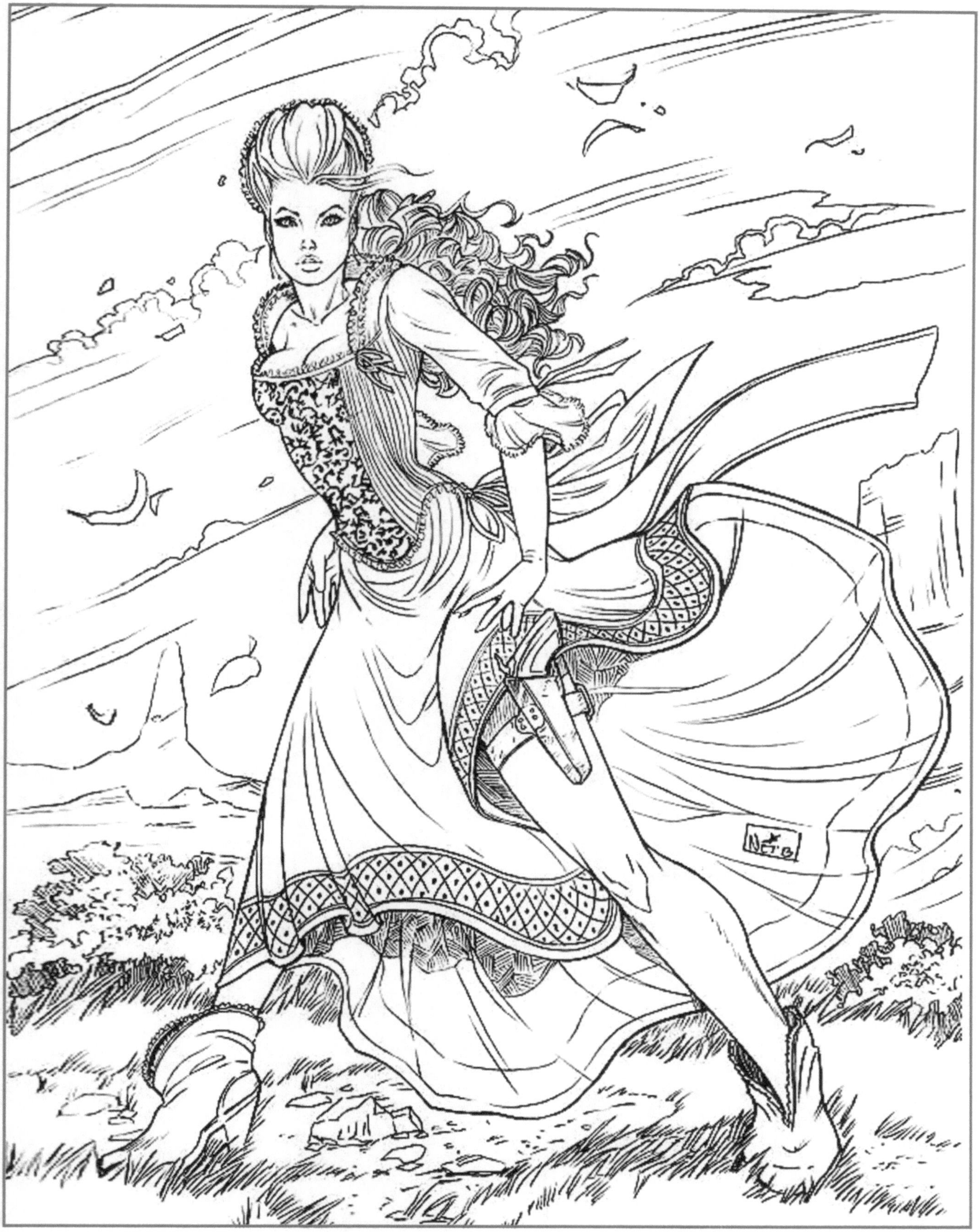

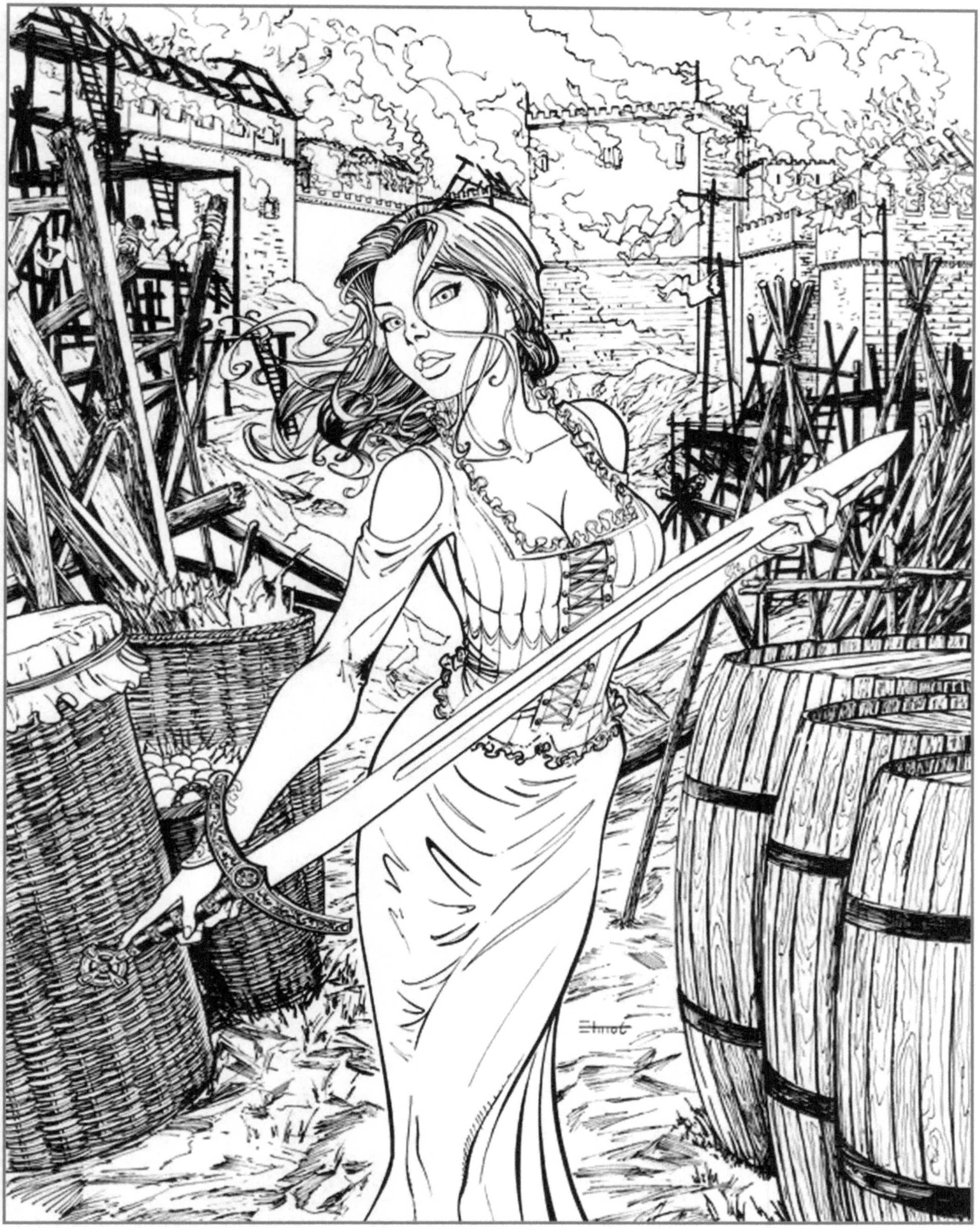

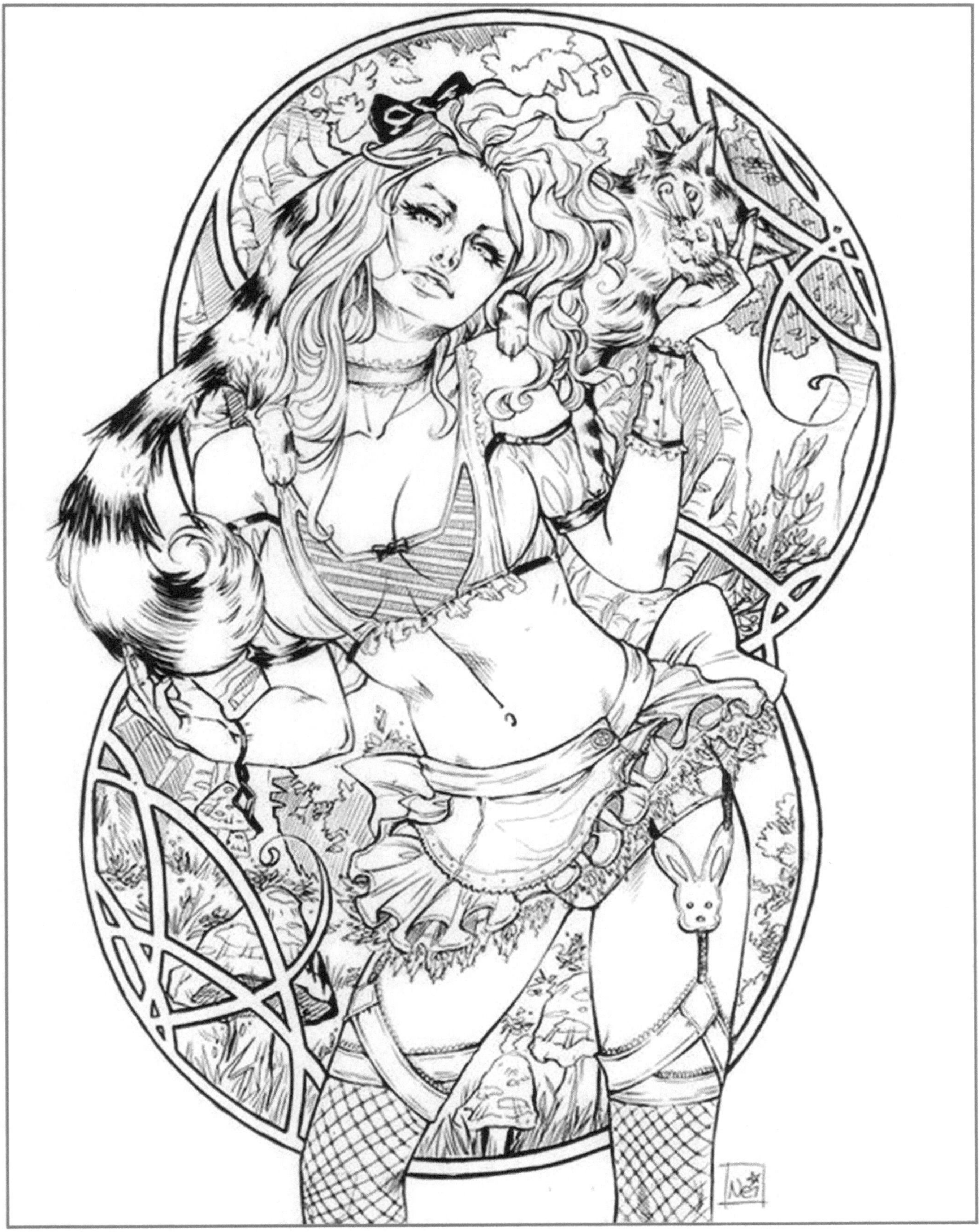
Nei

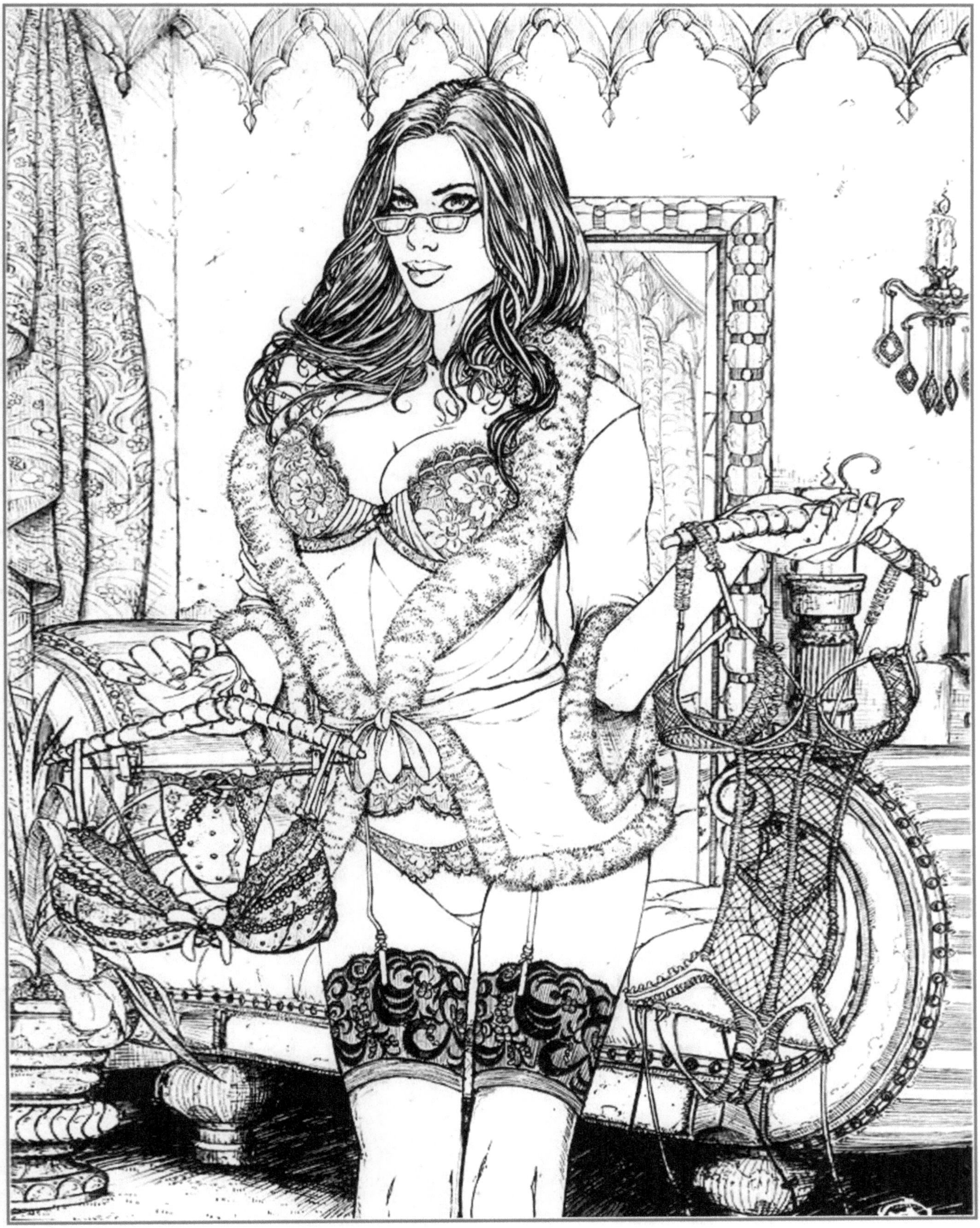

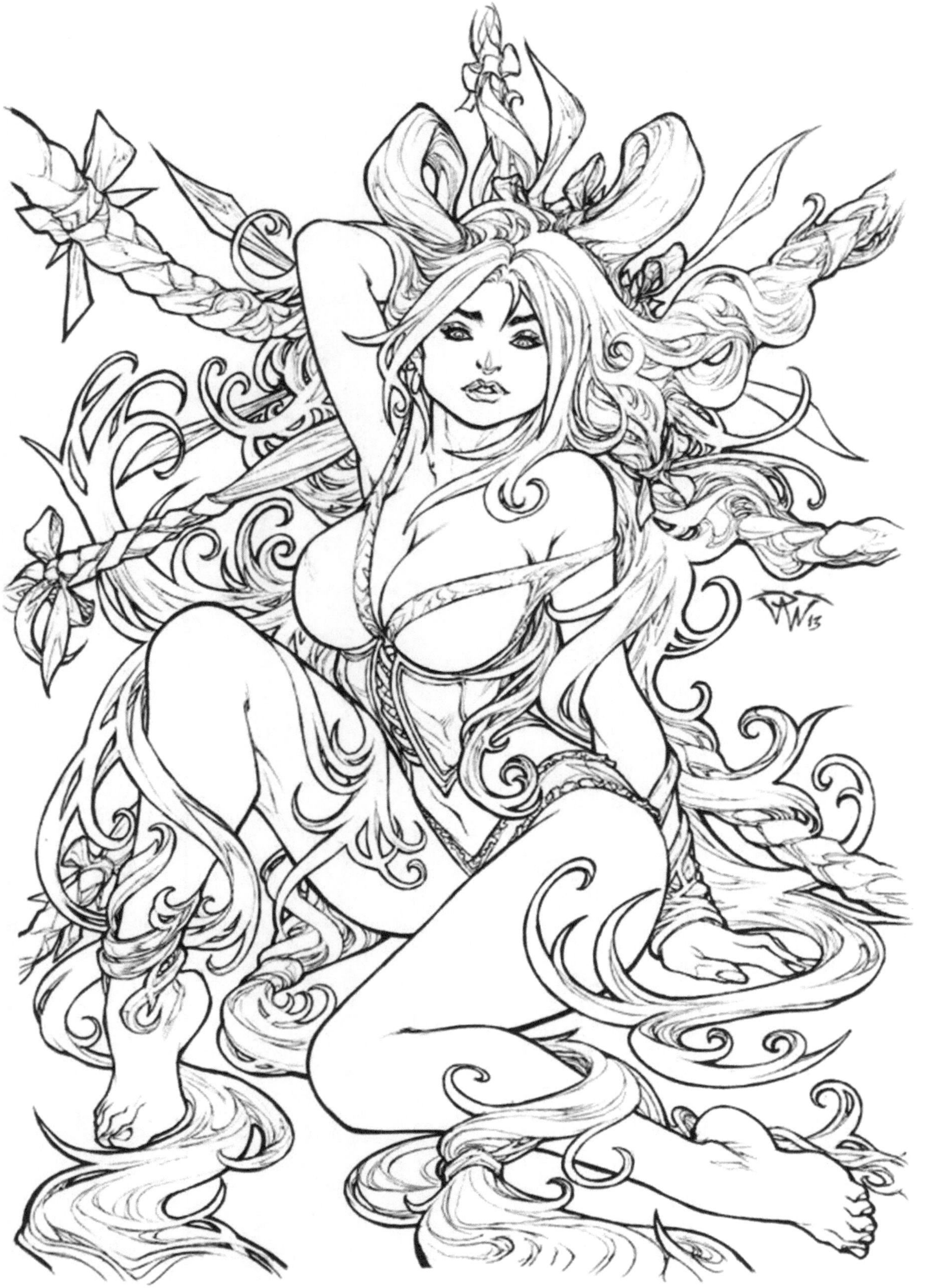

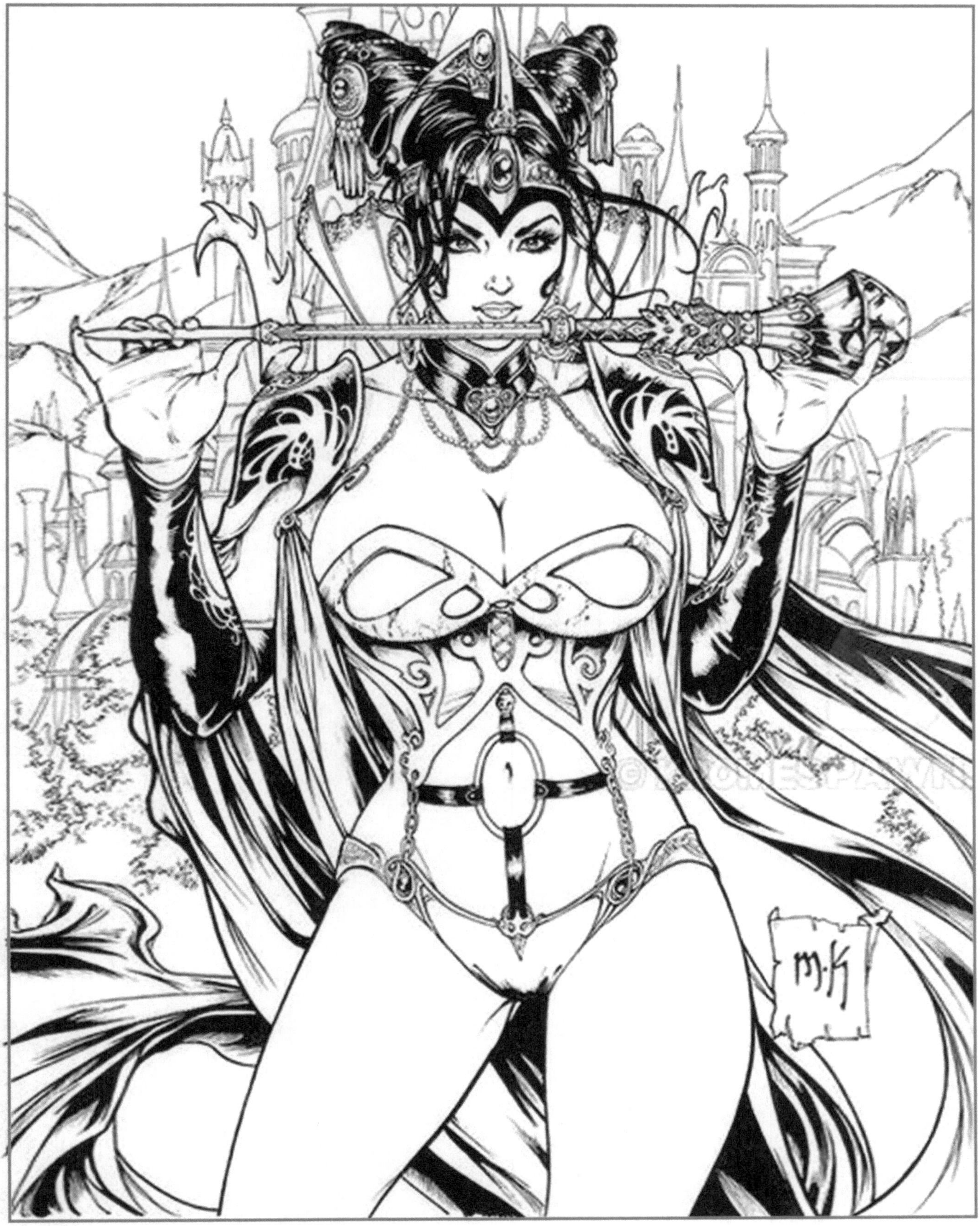
M.K

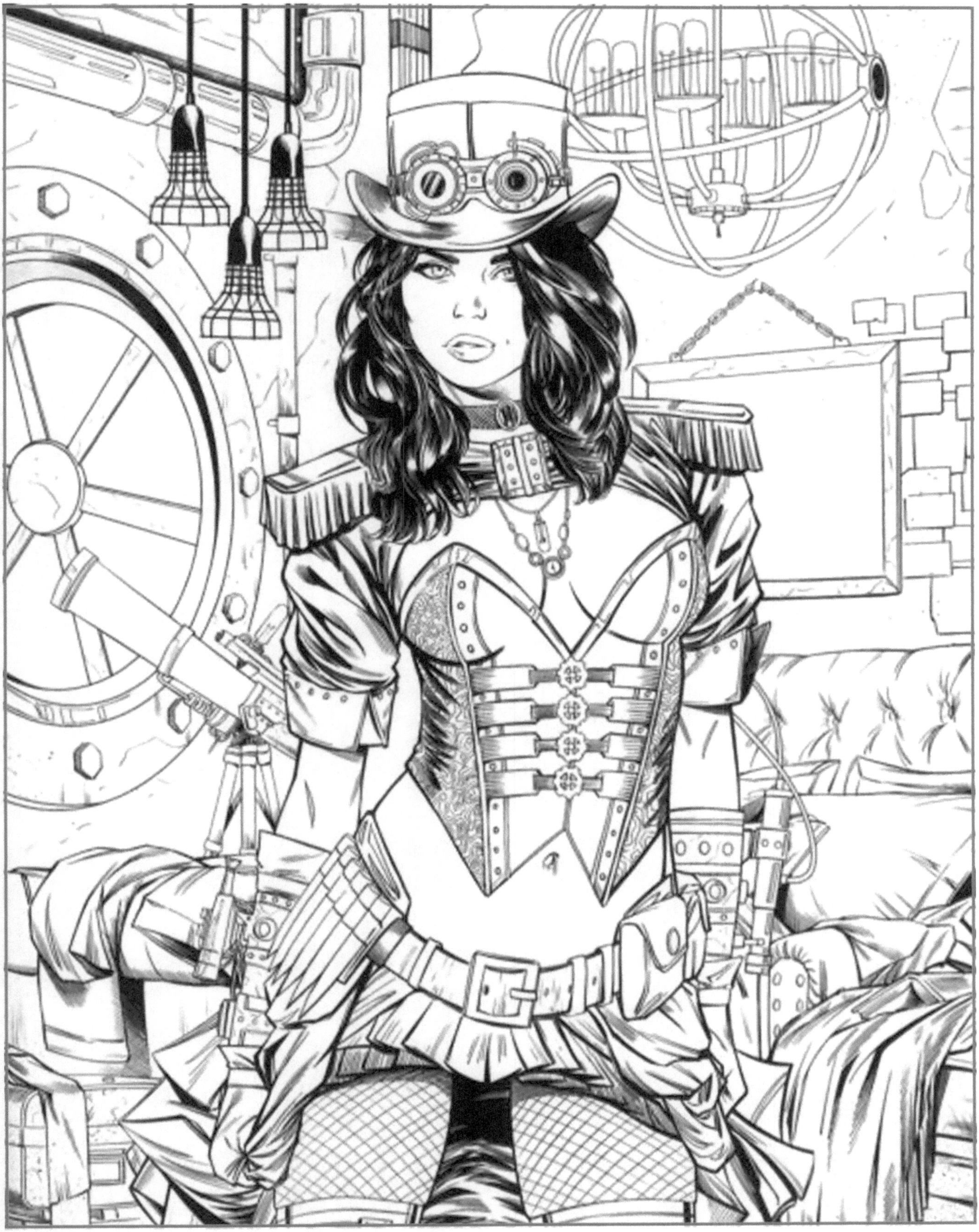

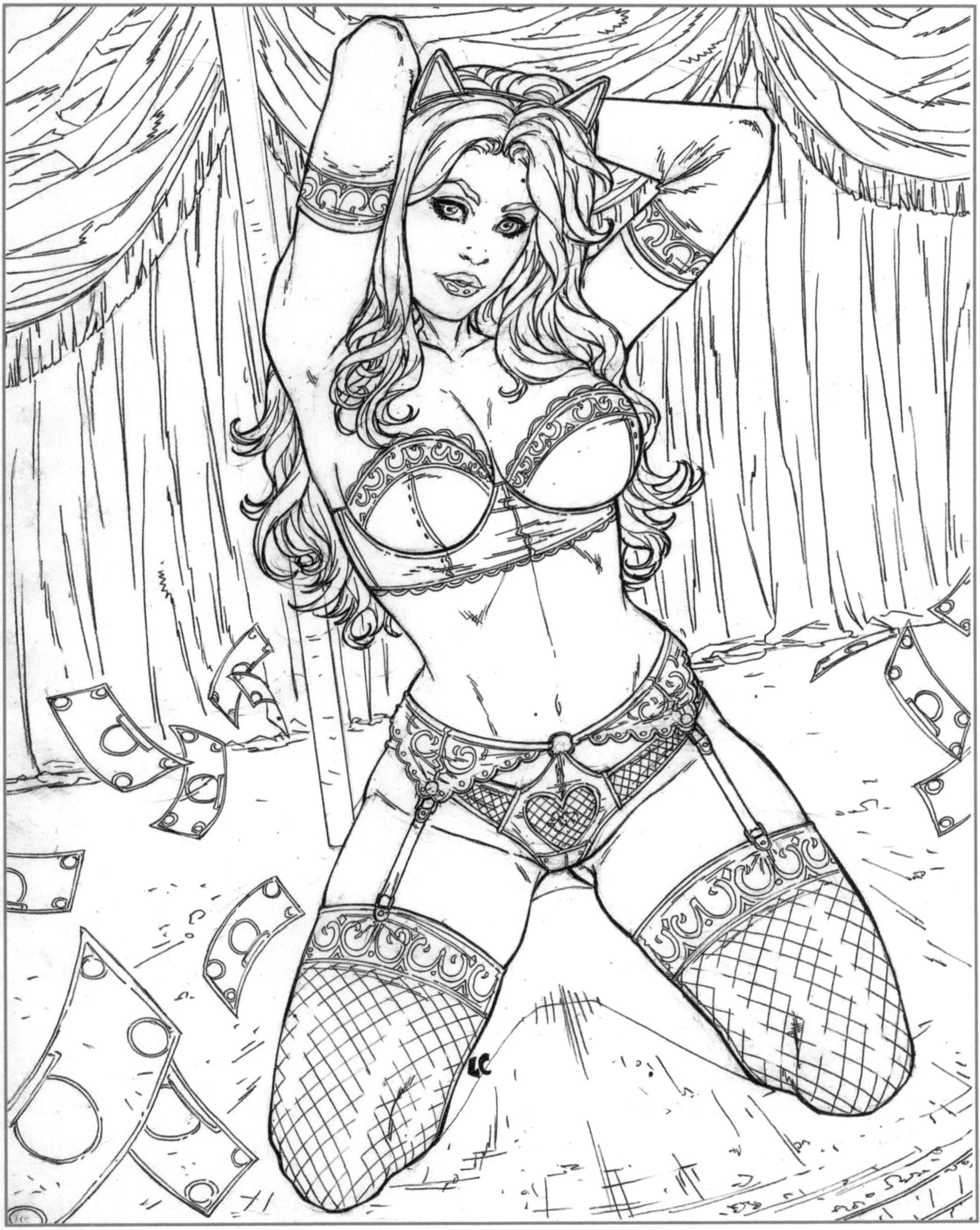

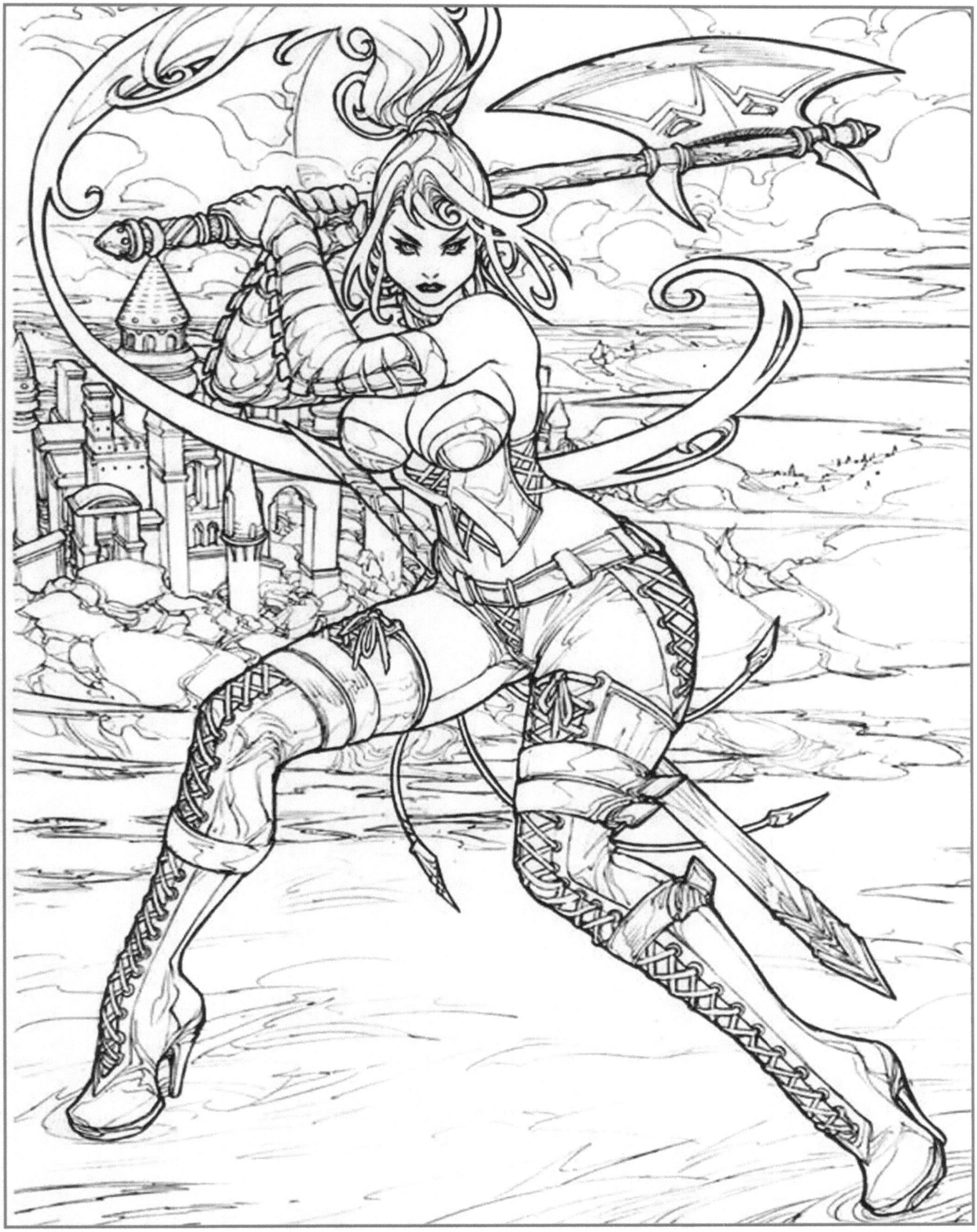

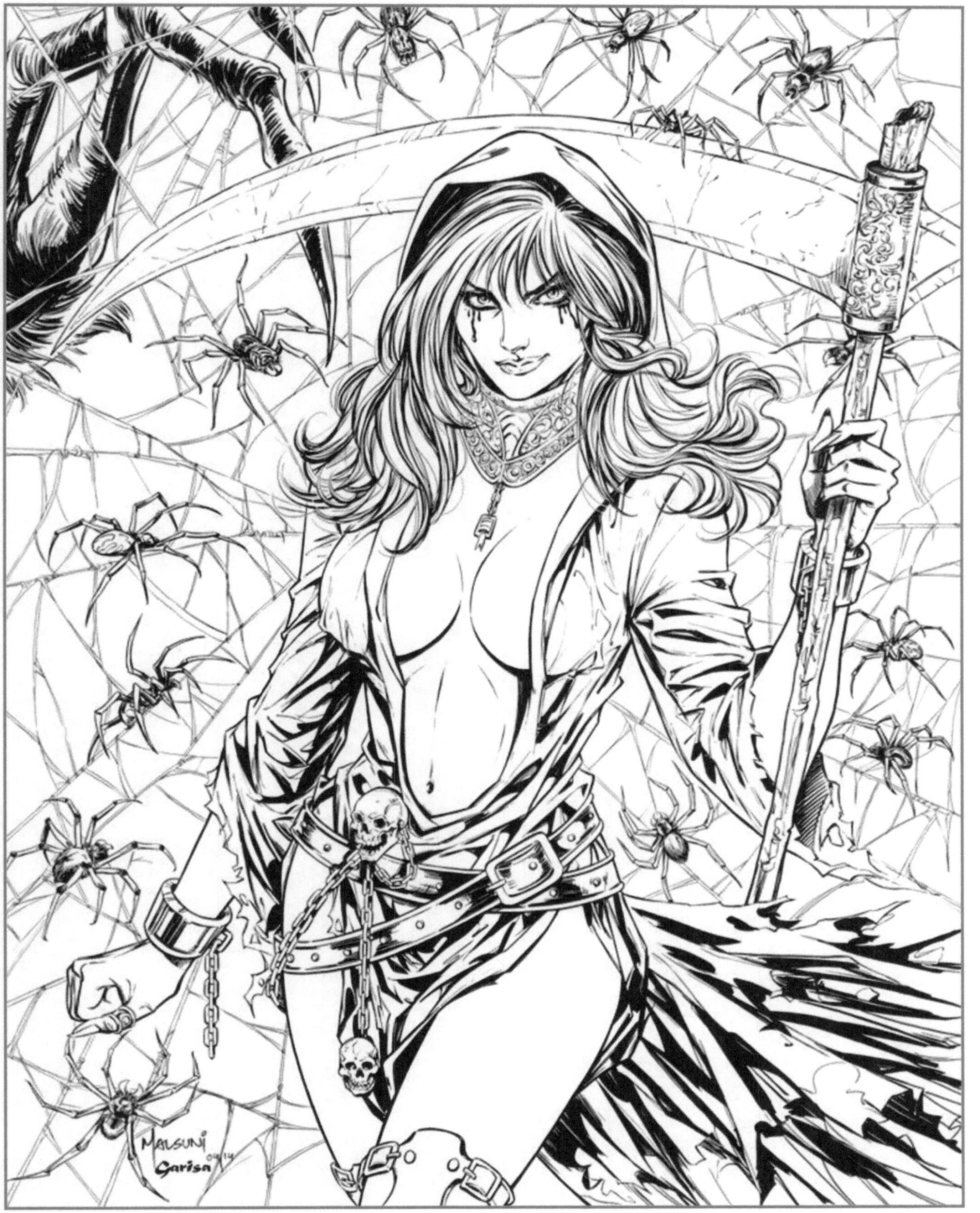
MALSUNI
04/14
Garisa

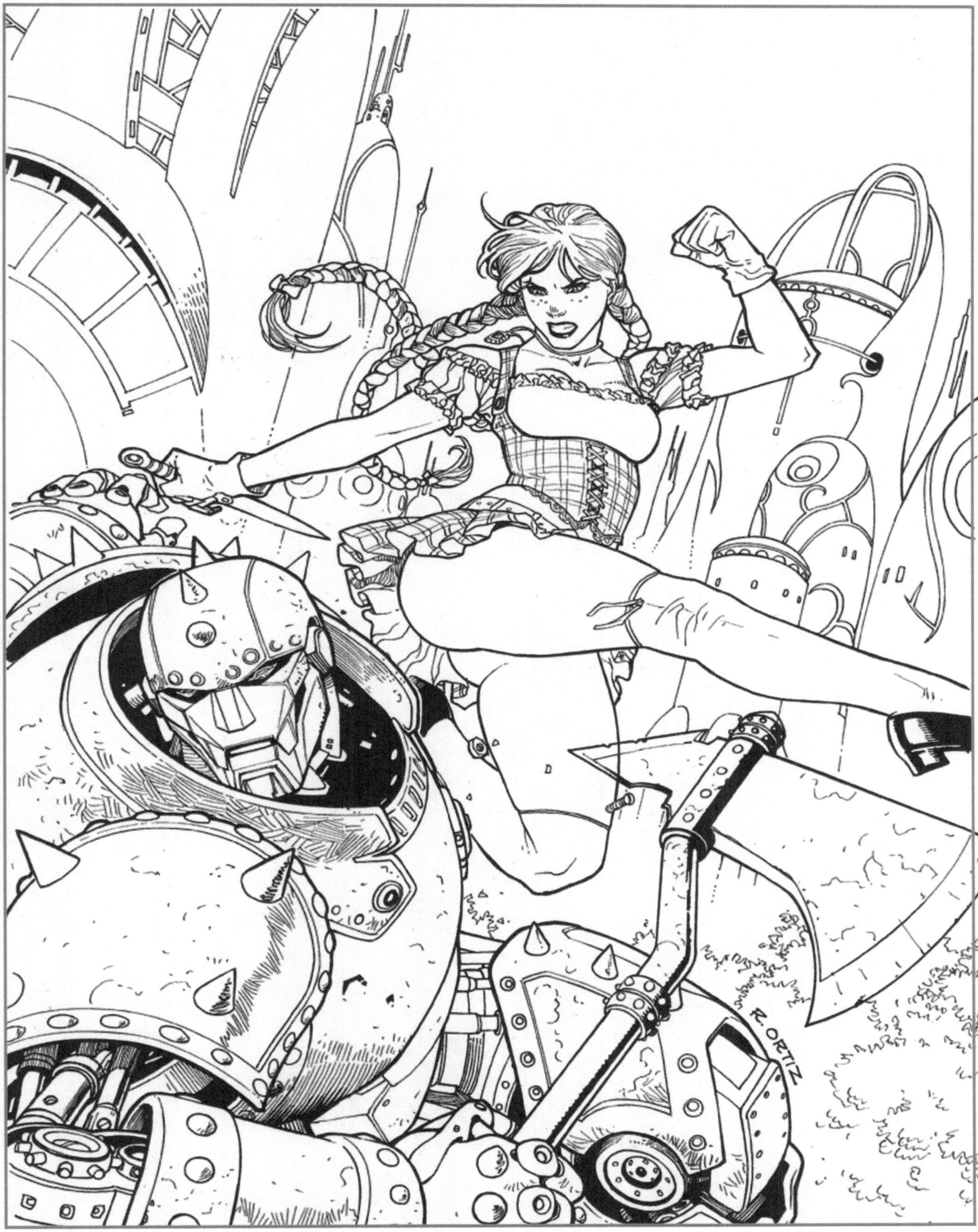
R. ORTIZ

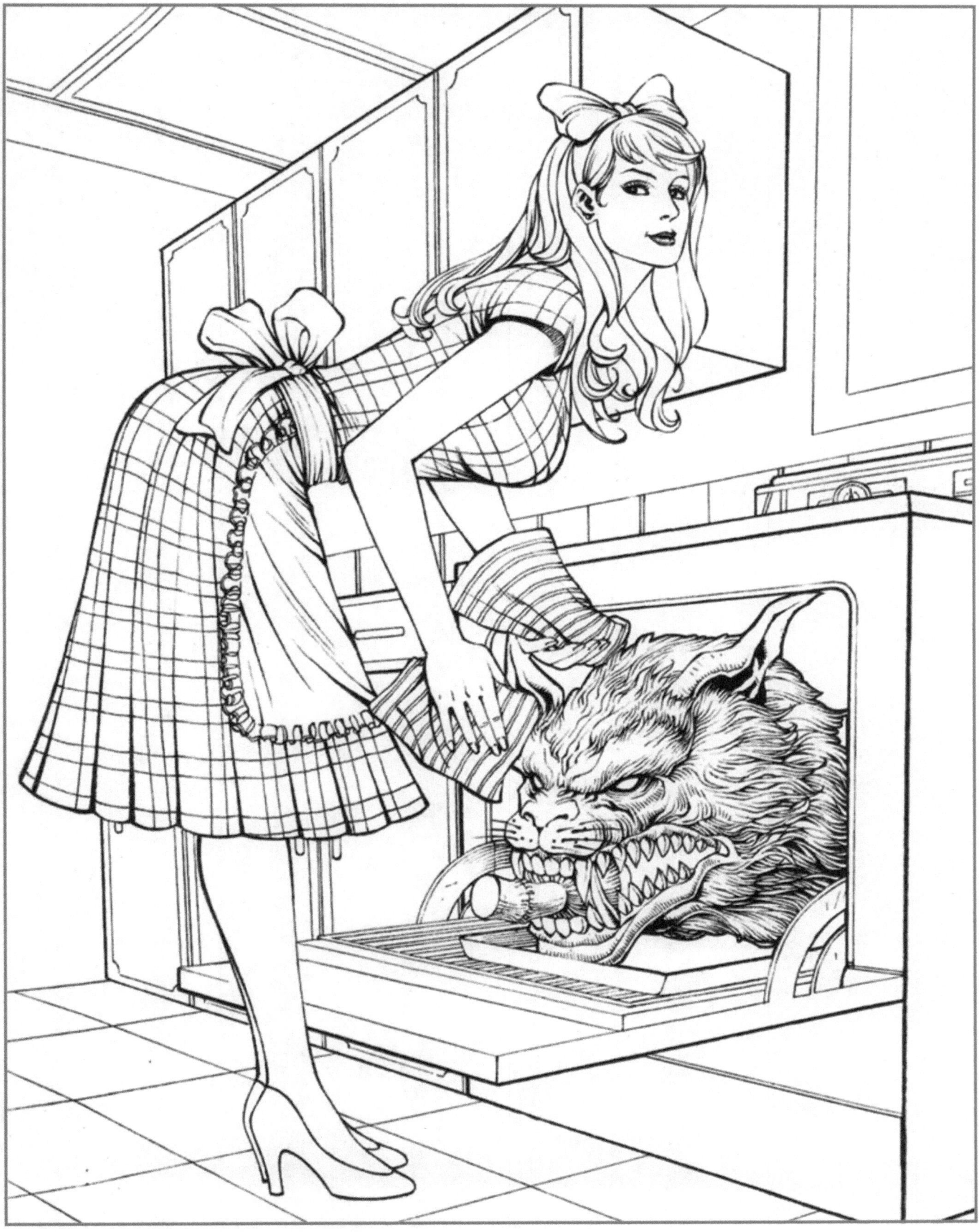

Made in United States
Troutdale, OR
11/07/2024